I DON'T REMEMBER DROPPING THE SKUNK BUT I DO REMEMBER TRYING TO BREATHE

I DON'T REMEMBER DROPPING THE SKUNK BUT I DO REMEMBER TRYING TO BREATHE

SURVIVAL SKILLS FOR TEENAGERS

KEN DAVIS

ZondervanPublishingHouse

Grand Rapids, Michigan

A Division of HarperCollinsPublishers

I Don't Remember Dropping the Skunk,
But I Do Remember Trying to Breathe
Survival Skills for Teenagers
Copyright © 1990 by Ken Davis
All rights reserved

Requests for information should be addressed to:
Zondervan Publishing House
1415 Lake Drive S.E., Grand Rapids, Michigan 49506

Davis, Ken, 1932–
    I don't remember dropping the skunk, but I do remember trying to breathe /
Ken Davis.
      p.   cm.
    Summary: Presents survival skills in a humorous fashion for teenagers
trying to live a Christian life.
    ISBN 0-310-32341-X
    1. Teenagers—Religious life. 2. Christian life—1960—Juvenile litera-
ture.   [1. Christian life.]   I. Title.
    BV4531.2.D38   1990
    248.8'3—dc20   90-38963
                                                    CIP
                                                    AC

Edited by David Lambert
Designed by The Church Art Works, Salem, Oregon
Cover illustration by Dave Adamson
Book illustration by Rand Kruback

Printed in the United States of America

91 92 93 94 95 / DP / 8 7 6 5 4

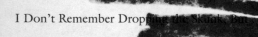

I Don't Remember Dropping the Skunk, But

CONTENTS

CHAPTER

1

DISCOVERING
THE REAL
YOU

I know that God does miracles because in 1964 I experienced one: I graduated from high school.

As I stood to get my diploma, there were twenty-five of my classmates sitting on the stage. None of them were really my friends. Several of the boys had enjoyed beating me up during the past four years, and I had never dated any of the girls. I didn't feel important, and I certainly didn't feel lovable. For me, holding that diploma was the culmination of some of the most difficult years of my life.

I weighed about 125 pounds, and I had curvature of the bone in both arms—not a severe handicap, but I was skinny and uncoordinated enough that I was poor in sports. I felt very unpopular. I had spent years trying to be something I wasn't —because I had no idea who I was.

But in the last two years of high school, something happened that would later change my life forever. An English teacher and some staff workers from Youth for Christ helped me begin to discover the real me. What a difference those people made in my life! My only wish is that it had happened earlier. Maybe it *can* happen earlier for you.

That's why I wrote this chapter—to help you discover who you are and to get you started on the road to liking the real you.

Know Who You Are

I always wanted to be an athlete. When I was real small, my hero was the ultimate athlete: Superman. One day I stole a pair of my sister's red underwear (please don't ever tell Superman), put on a bright blue T-shirt, and tied a flower-print dish towel around my neck for a cape.

As I stood in front of the mirror, with a big fan positioned to blow ripples of power into the dish towel, I suddenly knew my calling. Superman hadn't been seen for years—I was the one who would carry on the struggle for truth, justice, and the American way. It didn't matter that I only weighed fifty pounds soaking wet or that I had curvature of the bone in both arms. That was the Clark Kent part of me. The *real* me was standing before the mirror, ready to deal with the bullies in school and to show the kids on the ball team that they should have picked me.

Because I was new to the Superman business, I figured I needed a little help with my first attempt at flying, so I opened my bedroom window and climbed up on the dresser. With my dish-towel cape flowing behind me, I took off.

I still have a scar between my eyes where my head hit the steel frame of the bed.

When the bleeding stopped, I decided to let someone else be Superman. Instead, I would become the world's skinniest athlete.

I was a disaster. Did you know that it is possible to stop a hockey puck by catching it in your mouth? I found this out when they made me play goalie because I couldn't skate. For a week my top lip looked like an overripe zucchini.

It seemed like every sport I tried ended in embarrassment and failure. While skiing in Colorado, I fell in the ski line. In the chain reaction that followed, about fifty people fell like dominoes. And none of them were happy dominoes. I didn't want anyone to know I was responsible, so I just lay on the ground yelling, "Who fell?"

Later that day, I discovered that when you begin skiing down a 13,000-foot mountain, it is important to know how to stop.

On another occasion, while water-skiing in Northern Minnesota, I neglected to let go of the rope when I fell. I was dragged through the water like some giant fishing lure. I lost my swimming suit. My friends were puzzled when I refused to get in the boat. They offered to throw me a rope, but I didn't need a rope—I needed a wardrobe.

I could have just enjoyed the pure fun of these sports, but I didn't—I took these perfectly normal defeats very seriously. If I couldn't be an athlete, I didn't want to be anything at all. It never occurred to me that it might be okay to just be me.

Then someone came to my aid. In my senior year, an English teacher suggested that I go out for speech.

"Speech!" I said. "You've got to be kidding! All my friends are walking around school with letter jackets that have macho pictures on them—pictures of crossed hockey sticks, baseball bats, and footballs. I refuse to walk around school with a set of speech lips dangling from my jacket."

Fortunately, my teacher kept pestering me. I went out for speech and soon discovered I really enjoyed it. *Maybe*, I began to think, *God made me different—and maybe it's okay to be different*. I wasn't born to run touchdowns or leap tall buildings with a single bound. God gives wide receivers good hands, track stars good legs, weight lifters good muscles, and movie stars good looks. God gave me good lips.

Now, after all these years, I am finally having a letter jacket made. In the upper-right-pocket area, I will proudly display a big set of red lips.

Don't Try to Be a Duck

One of my favorite stories is "The Ugly Duckling." A swan is born into a family of ducks and lives the early years of his life in shame and sorrow because he feels ugly. He doesn't look or sound like the other ducks. But in the end, he realizes that he's really a *swan*— and then he doesn't have to try to be a duck anymore.

I meet a lot of miserable kids who try to be ducks when they're really swans or hawks or eagles. What kind of bird are you?

The first step in discovering the real you is to **know for sure who you aren't.** Next time you're with your friends, look around. You aren't any of the people you see, and you never will be. You may have some of their qualities, and you may even look a little like some of them, but you will never be just like them—and to try would be a tragic waste of time. Just like the snowflake, you are unique. Before the foundation of the world was laid, God had your picture hanging on his wall. You were created wonderful—and you were created one of a kind.

> For you created my inmost being; you knit me together in my mother's womb. I praise you because I am fearfully and wonderfully made; your works are wonderful, I know that full well. My frame was not hidden from you when I was made in the secret place. When I was woven together in the depths of the earth, your eyes saw my unformed body. All the days ordained for me were written in your book before one of them came to be. *Psalm 139:13-16*

> Praise be to the God and Father of our Lord Jesus Christ, who has blessed us in the heavenly realms with every spiritual blessing in Christ. For he chose us in him before the creation of the world to be holy and blameless in his sight. In love . . . *Ephesians 1:3-4*

Why, then, do we spend so much time comparing

ourselves to others?

"I wish I had her figure!"

"I wish I had his athletic ability."

"I wish I had her intelligence."

And on and on. Could it be because we think it's not cool to be different? After all, we're pressured to be like everybody else. We dress in the same styles, wear our hair the same way, and even use the same "hip" language. Then we shut out people who don't conform.

It's hard to know who you are when you live in a culture that insists on conformity. The world tells you what a duck is supposed to look like and then persuades you to be a duck like everybody else.

How powerful are these pressures to conform? That was graphically illustrated to me when I met Bill. The left side of Bill's head was shaved completely bald. But on the right side, his hair was about shoulder length—and right in the middle was a stiffly sprayed mohawk that divided the two halves. When I asked him about his unique hairstyle, Bill proudly explained how he fixed his hair and described the painstaking care necessary to keep it that way. Then he explained at great length that this hairdo was a symbol of his individuality, of his refusal to conform, of his independence.

Then I asked if he would ever consider going back to a more conventional hairstyle. His response was immediate: No, he would never go back to a more conventional hairstyle because none of the group he now associated with wore their hair that way.

Do you see the irony in his response? In his quest to be himself, Bill had merely switched the group he wanted to please. I couldn't help but wonder who the real Bill was.

And Bill's story is not rare; *many* men and women deny

who they are in order to fit in. Intelligent young women pretend to be dumb because they think that's what is expected of them. Creative young men suppress their sensitivity because it's not considered manly.

You'll never discover the real you as long as you keep comparing yourself with those around you. God didn't make people in batches. He gave you all of his attention and the best of his creativity. Don't ask, "What do my friends expect? What does the world want me to be?" Instead ask, "What did God create me to be?"

Go to a mirror and take a good long look at yourself. Look at the color of your hair and the build of your body. Look at that marvelous, one-of-a-kind face. Take in every little detail. Then look directly into those eyes and say out loud, "Hello, me." (One little suggestion: You might want to have the bathroom door locked when you do this. It would be discouraging to be taken away in a little white truck just as you were getting comfortable with who you are.)

Will you like everything you see? Probably not. That's okay. Right now it's important for you to realize that the "me" you are looking at is you. You may think you ought to lose some weight, clear up a few of the pimples, and fix the hair differently, but basically, what you see is what you get. If you're ready to accept that, you are well on your way to becoming everything God made you to be.

Ask God for Help

The second step in discovering the real you is to seek the help of your Creator.

"My Creator!" you scream. "It's his fault I'm the way I am!"

I understand that feeling. My mom made me go to

church every time the doors were open. Even if the doors were accidentally left unlocked, Mom would find out and take me to church. One of those times I walked into my Sunday school class just as the teacher said, "God made you."

My mouth dropped open. Finally I had found the person responsible for this skinny excuse for a body. If God was a loving God, why did he make me this way?

I wondered whether there had been an industrial accident in heaven that day. Or maybe God had decided to do a new experiment. I could just picture him, mixing together some strange new chemicals in a Frankenstein-like laboratory. Then, as I emerged from the steam, God said in thunderous tones: "Oops!"

No, I thought, God would never experiment with the people he loved—so he must have just made a mistake. As all the humans were passing on a conveyer belt, God was passing out athletic ability, good looks, super charm—and just as I approached, he sneezed, and I slipped by with nothing of value.

I have good news. God did not goof when he made me, and he didn't goof when he made you. He knew exactly what he was doing. You are his rare and priceless creation.

Remember, there is a lot about you that can't be seen in a mirror. Your emotional and spiritual makeup are just as important as the body that they come in. You can see the outside body by looking in the mirror, but how do you discover the real person who lives in there?

Ask the Creator.

Two years ago, I considered buying an airplane called a Maul. But before I bought one, I wanted to find out as much about this airplane as I could. Many of the articles I had read gave conflicting reports. One man told me he wouldn't own one if it was given to him, but another claimed it was the best airplane of its kind in the world. If I couldn't find dependable information on how this plane was made and what it was capable of doing, how could I decide whether to buy one?

Finally, out of desperation, I called the factory in Georgia. Do you know who answered the phone? None other than the inventor, Mr. Maul himself. He had dreamed of this airplane before it existed; he had planned out its creation on paper and built it from scratch. He knew everything there was to know about the Maul, right down to the last nut and bolt. Before I got off the phone I knew what made the Maul different from all the other planes that flew. Mr. Maul, the inventor, had answered all my questions.

With all of the conflicting input you get, it can be difficult to know who you really are. Your friends want you to be a duck, your parents insist that you're a weasel, and you want to be a tiger. Why not talk to the Inventor? Why not talk to the one who dreamed of you before the world existed, who made a blueprint like no other in the universe, who created you from scratch and then destroyed the mold?

Your creator doesn't want you to go through life frustrated about who you are. It's your fear of being different, of being rejected, that causes the real you to be shoved into the center of a big onion with many layers of protection. Ask God to help you peel away the layers so that you can see the beauty of his true creation. Ask him to give you the courage to be yourself without the fear of rejection. He wants you to know the real you. He invented you with a special purpose in mind, and he can free you to fulfill that purpose.

Find the Clues to the Real You

The third step is to ask yourself some specific questions that will help reveal the real you.

The first question is: **What are you good at?**

The natural athlete finds it easy to catch a fly ball, run with blazing speed, or master the parallel bars. The natural actor has the ability to mimic others' voices or gestures, or to believably communicate the emotion of a character; the artist can, through paints, clay, or some other medium, capture the beauty she sees around her. Others find it easy to talk with people and make friends. Still others know how to show love and care for people in need.

All of these abilities are gifts from God. Now—what are *you* good at?

"Well," you might be saying, "I'm not really good at anything." If that's your response, then the list of skills and abilities you admire is too short. There are *lots* of important skills, but most of us never think beyond a few highly visible ones — athletic ability, art, music, acting, or public performance —because those are the abilities that are held in high esteem by our culture. People gifted in those areas get the most attention.

But God never made a good-for-nothing. Everyone is good at something.

One day I was talking with a seventeen-year-old girl named Karen. She told me how terrible she felt because she wasn't good at anything. During our entire conversation, Karen was babysitting her little sister Beth. When I had showed up at their house, she had asked me to wait a few minutes until she finished reading a story to this beautiful child. Then, as we talked, she continued to show love and concern for her sister. Several times during our conversation, she paused to answer a question or play a little game with Beth.

I'm sure Karen thought I was changing the subject

when I asked how she could keep her little sister entertained so easily. Her face brightened as she told me how much she loved little kids. She told me her friends thought she was crazy because she actually *enjoyed* babysitting. "Little kids are people too," she said. "It's important to make them feel worthwhile."

I just smiled. "Karen," I said, "God has given you a marvelous ability that you'll be able to use all your life. You are gifted at working with little kids, and you *enjoy* doing it. That gift is worth every bit as much as being a good dancer, or actor, or gymnast." For the first time Karen saw that she did have some special abilities. She had the potential to affect the lives of hundreds of children.

The second question is: **What do you enjoy doing?**

God made you to enjoy doing what he gifted you to do. One of the reasons so many people are dissatisfied with their lives is that they're not doing what God created them to do.

Even if your talent isn't likely to win the admiration of your friends, you'll be much happier if you do what you know you were designed to do. If you try to make a toy poodle be a sled dog, you'll have one very unhappy poodle—and a slow-moving sled. That's because toy poodles were bred to sit around looking like a minor explosion in a Q-tip box. They enjoy barking at nothing and listening to their owners say things like, "Oh, what a cute poopsie—come to Mama." I don't particularly like poodles, but they don't care what I think. Being pampered makes poodles very happy.

Recently, in Alaska, I became acquainted with the Alaskan husky. *This* is a real sled dog. If you say, "Oh, what a cute poopsie—come to Mama," to an Alaskan husky he'll probably take a cute bite out of you. Alaskan huskies are bred to pull sleds. This dog becomes wild with excitement when he realizes that he's going to be hooked to a sled. Barking and yelping his desire to be on the trail, he is almost uncontrollable as he's being attached to the harness. When the musher gives the signal to go, these beautiful dogs run with outright joy. Tongues hanging out to one side, they seem to be smiling as they fully enjoy what they were created to do. They don't care if poodles think they're stupid or if a Great Dane calls them sissy. They love to run so much that some have been known to run until they drop.

What do you enjoy doing? What activities bring you feelings of accomplishment and fulfillment? Those are the skills and talents you were born to use. One of the greatest joys in life comes from recognizing that and then diving in head first to be all God created you to be.

Like the Alaskan husky, run till you drop.

Give It Back to the Creator

The fourth step is to put all of what you find into God's hands. Let the inventor control the machine.

Burt Rutan is probably one of the greatest aviation inventors in recent history. Over the years, most airplane manufacturers have stayed with the same basic designs. But Burt Rutan's airplanes don't look like any airplanes you've ever seen. And they fly better. He builds airplanes with a set of wings in the front and the propeller in the back. As a result of his ingenuity, the Rutan airplanes are among the fastest and most economical in the world.

Burt set out to create an airplane that could fly around the world without stopping. When the Voyager took off on the beginning of its journey, the wings were so heavy with fuel that the ends scraped the ground, and the very ends of the wings ripped off. But Burt Rutan, who was piloting the

Voyager, continued the flight anyway; his intimate knowledge of this airplane told him that, even with the winglets gone, the flight would still be possible.

Burt and his copilot Jana Yeager, overcoming incredible odds, traveled completely around the world in the Voyager and then landed successfully. They had accomplished something that no one had ever done before. And the *only* person on the face of the earth who could have flown that airplane around the world was the inventor, Burt Rutan. Only he knew how to get the best performance from his creation. When the engine failed over the ocean, he knew how to restart it. He knew how to make the airplane accomplish the purpose for which it was created. This airplane now hangs in the Smithsonian Institute as a reminder of what can be done when a machine is built with purpose and the designer uses the machine to accomplish that purpose.

Your creator designed you with a purpose much more profound than any machine. Within the boundaries of your lifelong mission to glorify him are unlimited opportunities for unique service. It really doesn't matter how much wealth you accumulate or how much power you wield. It doesn't matter what "hall of fame" you are in or how popular you are. What matters is that you live to the fullest the potential for which you were created.

At fifteen, Ted Place gave his life to Jesus Christ. Because of the great sacrifice God had made for him, Ted wanted to give something back—but he felt he had nothing to give. He was the shortest kid in his class, he stuttered when he talked, and he had such low self esteem that he turned beet red whenever the teachers called on him.

There was only one thing that Ted was really good at. He could turn somersaults better than anyone around. Since that was all he had to give, Ted gratefully gave it all to the Lord.

The next day he went to the park to use this ability for God. In the middle of an open field, he began to turn somersaults. Soon a crowd of children gathered to watch. Impressed with his skill, they asked Ted how he had learned to tumble so well. He showed them how to do some simple tumbling tricks—and then, at the coaxing of the Holy Spirit, Ted took a deep breath and said, "I want to tell you something —I'm a Christian."

Ted had expected that the kids would run away, or maybe laugh at him. Instead, a boy asked, "What do you mean you're a Christian?" Ted told them how he had given his life to Christ, and then he invited his new friends to church.

Encouraged, the next day Ted went looking for more kids. Wherever he found a group of children, he would do somersaults and tumbling maneuvers and then tell the kids about the love of Jesus Christ.

Ted didn't realize until many years later that God was doing a special miracle in his life. God had asked for the only skill Ted had: tumbling. When Ted was faithful in giving God his somersaults, God began to develop another talent Ted didn't even know he had. As he told hundreds of kids about the love of Christ, God was developing Ted's speaking ability. What started as a fifteen-year-old boy giving God his ability to do somersaults, snowballed into a full and exciting life of ministry that influenced the lives of thousands of people around the world. My own life is included in that list.

Today, Ted Place runs a counseling ministry that brings the healing power of Christ to families that are experiencing difficulty. The lives he has touched cannot be counted. And all because, at fifteen, he was willing to give God a gift that the world didn't value much. He gave God his

Discovering the Real You

somersaults.

The Bible is full of wonderful examples of people like Ted. David was good at guarding sheep and shooting a slingshot. God used those abilities to bring down the giant Goliath and save the Israelites. Moses stuttered and was basically a chicken, yet God chose him to lead his people out of captivity to the Promised Land.

First, discover who you are and what you can do. Then, give those abilities to God.

Let the one who invented you decide how you should be used.

CHAPTER
2

LEARNING TO LOVE YOURSELF

I gazed into the green eyes now only inches from my face. Nervously, I glanced down at the lips approaching mine. Finally, at the last possible moment, I closed my eyes and puckered up. My lips touched gently at first, and then with firm passion.

But when I pulled away, there was no one there—only my own reflection made fuzzy by the greasy lip smears on the mirror.

I was practicing, just in case someday I might encounter the real thing.

When I suggest that you learn to love yourself, I'm not advocating long necking sessions with the mirror or developing a romantic feeling toward yourself. But I do believe that, until you learn to love yourself, you'll have a very hard time loving God or loving others.

The second greatest killer of teenagers is suicide. Why? In many cases, it's because these unfortunate teens lack feelings of self-worth. That same lack of self-worth causes other teens to give in to peer pressure. It keeps others from seeking God—because, after all, why would he want anything to do with them?

I used to think that I was the only one who struggled with a lack of self-worth; I thought other people felt pretty good about themselves. Then, as I began to speak around the country, I discovered that thousands of teenagers and adults suffer from the same disease. I met cheerleaders, football heroes, academic whizzes, popular kids as well as unpopular kids who did not like themselves and were convinced that their lives were of little value.

The belief that your life has no value is a lie straight from the pit of hell. It leads to self hatred, depression, sin, and death. It does little good to discover who you really are if you have nothing but contempt for the person you find. The question then is, "How do I learn to like myself?" It isn't as easy as going back into the bathroom, looking in the mirror, and saying, "I like you." It takes time, understanding, and effort. This chapter will show you how.

Use the Right Ruler

One of the reasons we don't like ourselves is that we measure our self-worth with the wrong ruler.

If the only reason you can find for liking yourself is your ability to play football, then what happens when you can no longer play? If your self-worth depends on a relationship with another person, then what happens when that relationship crumbles? I'm always greatly saddened when I hear about teenagers who have taken their own lives because a boy or girl friend left them. Your value goes far beyond any single relationship—or any ability. In the previous chapter, I tried to help you find out who you are by identifying your gifts and abilities. But remember this: *Your personal worth goes beyond all of those abilities put together.*

Dave Burnham was an all-state championship football player looking forward to scholarships at the college of his choice. His personal worth was based on his ability to play football. As Dave puts it, "Football was my god." His senior year, in the middle of an important game, Dave was hit by a very solid linebacker. When he regained consciousness he was under the bleachers on a stretcher. He couldn't talk or move his hands or legs. As his dad leaned over him and whispered a verse from the Bible, Dave was suddenly very aware that his god was too small. The football he worshiped was not with him now. From where he lay at the back of the stadium, Dave could hear the people cheering as the game that had become his whole life went on without him. Dave decided then that he needed a bigger God. He needed a reason for living; he needed a sense of self-worth that was bigger than just the game of football. With the same determination that made him a great football player, Dave Burnham began his search for a God that would not leave him and a purpose for living that could not be taken away.

Twenty years ago, Dave's story affected my life as he told us how in Jesus Christ he had found a God that would not let him down. A God that gave life the kind of value and meaning that could not be taken away. As I write this, I have just spoken to Dave on the phone. He told me that just a few days ago he stood on the very field where that injury occurred to film a television show that would tell his story once again. We hadn't seen each other in years, but that conversation revealed that God has not let him down.

If your self-worth is wrapped up in your talent, popularity, or wealth, I pray with all my heart that you will discover the one God that brings priceless value to every life and makes every moment worth living.

In contrast to Dave's life, consider the following: At the height of his career, on January 28, 1977, comedian Freddie Prinze took his own life. He had everything most people can only dream of: all the money he could spend, national popularity, and a successful acting career. Something he said shortly before he died is particularly revealing. In a moment of despondence, he said to a friend, "I can't hear them laughing anymore." Freddie had discovered that all of the laughter in the world couldn't bring him the personal worth or fulfillment that he sought.

For a while, laughter, fame, money, or recognition seems to cut it. But soon the truth works its way to the surface

What if I'm injured or broke; what if my friends leave me? If you believe the lie that fame, money, or personal skills give you worth, then when those things are gone, life will have lost its meaning. But wait— *it's a lie!* Your worth doesn't come from your popularity or your talent or your friends. It comes from a source that can't be destroyed or broken down, a source so powerful that not even you can destroy it.

You may be thinking, *Ken, if I love myself, isn't that being conceited?* The answer is no. The Bible encourages you to love yourself. Seven times in the New Testament God tells us to love our neighbor as we love ourselves. If you live by that principle, and if you think of yourself as a worthless worm, then I would rather not be your neighbor. On the other hand, if you recognize that you are a creation of God with priceless worth, I *want* to be your neighbor. Conceit is when people ignore God and act as though they deserve the credit for what God has given them.

Recognize Your Value in God's Eyes

At the core of your ability to love yourself is the recognition that God loves you.

I was reminded of his incredible love one night when I was putting my daughter to bed. Never, in all my life, have I laughed so hard. And in the midst of that joy, God reminded me of just how valuable my life is to him. Let me tell you the story:

"Go to bed," I said to my daughter. She was three years old at the time.

"Wait," she moaned. "Because I ... because ..."

I could almost see the wheels turning in her head as she stalled me with a whole string of unfinished sentences. "Go to bed," I repeated.

Her eyes brightened—she had thought of something. "No, wait, because I need to have a drink of water." She said it in a tone that indicated I should have known this in the first place. Now she was in full form.

"You can't have a drink of water."

"Why?"

"Because you've been wetting the bed."

"I quit," she responded in wide-eyed innocence.

I was a little angry now. "You didn't quit, Traci. In fact, you wet the bed just last night."

"The cat did that," she sputtered, casting an accusing look at the innocent little kitty curled up in the corner.

I couldn't believe I was arguing with a three year old. "Don't lie to me," I scolded. "The spot on your bed was bigger than a pizza. How can you blame that little bitty kitten?"

"It wasn't *our* cat," she lied, eyes still wide with innocence.

Then she started to tell me about a giant cat that had broken into her room and relieved himself on the bed. I managed to keep my composure long enough to give a one-sentence lecture on lying and set a time for further discussion. Then I relented and sent her to the bathroom for a drink of water. I went into the living room and rolled on the floor, laughing.

Ten minutes later I realized that she was still in the bathroom. I opened the door to discover she had been drinking water for ten minutes! Her little stomach was bloated. She looked like she was trying to smuggle a basketball somewhere.

"You get to bed right now!" I barked.

"I have to go bathroom," she said, looking as if she

might explode any moment. I had to let her go—or the giant cat would be back for sure.

When I looked up a few moments later, she had removed all her clothes and was standing in the hall. Evidently she had heard us laughing and had decided to switch tactics.

"Catch me!" she squealed as she ran past.

There is one thing a good dad cannot resist, and that is to chase his naked child. What I forgot is that God has given naked children the ability to turn on a dime. She went into the kitchen and made a sharp right. Up to that point I was right behind her, but I was wearing wool socks. Our kitchen has a linoleum floor. In the wild scramble to keep my balance while trying to make a sharp turn, I broke a blender, and as I lay on the floor she ran out the front door.

Now my child is running down the street without a stitch of clothes yelling, "Catch me, catch me." I was a few yards behind her yelling, "Come here, come here!" I just knew that the neighbors must be watching out their windows, shaking their heads. I caught her about a block away. It was only when I grabbed that giggling little body that I remembered I was wearing only that pair of wool socks and my underwear.

I scooped her up and ran back to the house, praying that I could make it before the neighbors could get their Polaroid cameras. Once inside, I thought I was going to die with laughter. It took several minutes to stop—each time we would think we were done, we would look at each other and start laughing all over again. Finally I grabbed my daughter, gave her a big hug, and sent her to bed. She went without a struggle. And just before she entered her room she turned to smile and giggle one more time. Then she quietly disappeared into the room.

I will remember that moment forever as one of the

happiest moments of my life. I was overwhelmed with the love I felt for my daughter and the unrestrained joy we had shared together that night. At that very moment God brought to my memory the Bible verse I had learned as a child, and tears of gratitude filled my eyes:

> But God demonstrates his own love for us in this: While we were still sinners, Christ died for us. *Romans 5:8*

You were valuable enough to God that he was willing to give the life of his only Son. As the dad of two children, I can tell you this: That price is higher than I would be willing to pay. I don't know your name or anything about you, yet I believe I would be willing to risk my life to save yours. But I could never give the lives of either of my children to save yours. I wouldn't do it even if you could convince me you deserved it.

Look at that verse again. God did for you what I could not bring myself to do. God loved you so much that he freely *gave his only Son* so that you might have eternal life. That's how much he valued your life. The Creator of the universe paid the highest price that can be paid to give you the chance to experience a personal relationship with God through Jesus Christ, to be totally forgiven of your sins, and to live forever. *You are priceless.* He knows both the bad and the good about you, and he still loves you.

Now it's time for *you* to love you.

Recognize That Loving Yourself Is Not Easy

Often, kids come to me after one of my shows and say, "It's easy for *you* to like yourself. You get to travel all over the world speaking and doing comedy. People like you; you've made a name for yourself."

I tell them that it isn't easy for me to like myself. The

good vibes that come with hearing an audience applaud and laugh, and the high that popularity and success bring, only last for a short period of time. Even after years of what most people would call a very successful career, I still don't find it easy to like myself. When I get up in the morning, the person who swings his feet out of bed is a scared little boy of 120 pounds, afraid of being beat up one more time. Satan begins his lies immediately, reminding me of those who have accomplished so much more than I have. "You're not famous," he taunts. "You'll never amount to anything." Many times I'm tempted to give up and settle for second best. Other times I'm tempted to struggle for more fame or fortune just to prove him wrong.

Do you know what saves me? What saves me is *the truth*. I break Satan's bony grip by remembering the truth. And the truth is that God loves me just the way I am. He loved me so much he gave his Son to die for me. Because of his love *I am priceless*. And because of his love so are you!

You see, when I look in the mirror, it's obvious the world wouldn't rate me as a ten for appearance. They wouldn't give my career a very high rating either. When I look in my own heart, I don't want anyone to know what the rating would be. But those aren't the rulers God uses to judge our worth. Everything you are right this moment was bought with a price. The price was the blood of Jesus Christ, the living Son of God. All of the money, laughter, success, popularity, or power in the world cannot bring me the fulfillment or worth that his love brings.

When Freddie Prinze said to his friend, "I can't hear them laughing anymore," I think what he really meant was, "Their laughter no longer makes me feel worthwhile." But the truth about God's love for you will always make you feel worthwhile. Learn to remember it and to believe it, no matter what lies you hear from anyone else.

Continually Review the Evidence of Your Worth

It is important to daily review the reasons for loving yourself. Whenever self-doubt begins to destroy your spirit, remember these truths.

Reasons to love yourself ...

1. God created you with meaning and purpose. You are not just some accident.

2. God created you unique. There is not another person like you on the face of the earth. You are one of a kind (like rare) and that makes you very valuable.

3. God gives you the opportunity to affect the lives of other human beings for eternity. You can bring the message of life to those who are spiritually dead.

4. Most importantly, God loved you and valued you so much that he gave his Son Jesus Christ so that you might be free from the penalty of sin to live forever with him. That makes you *priceless.*

Now—go back to the bathroom one more time, lock the door, and look in the mirror. What you see is of priceless value. (If you're not in the bathroom yet, *get in there*—this is very important.) Now look at the image in the mirror and say, "Hi, me." Go on; do it.

Now say to the person you see in the mirror, "Because God made you with purpose, you have value."

Now say, "Because God made you special you are a rare treasure and I like you."

"Because God has given you the responsibility and privilege of bringing others to eternal life, you have great worth."

"Because God loved you so much that he gave his son

for you, you are priceless."

That is the truth that will set you free to love yourself and those around you. You can leave the bathroom now—but never forget:

"Because of him, I am priceless!"

CHAPTER

3

KNOW WHAT
YOU
BELIEVE

One segment of the population I have always found intriguing is the "no opinion" segment reflected in national polls. When polls are taken on any specific subject, there is a substantial number of people who are for a particular issue, a substantial number who are against a particular issue, and a small group of people who have "no opinion." They don't know what they believe. I've often wondered what it would be like to be at a party with a group of these individuals.

"Hi, how are you?"

"I don't know."

"What did you think of the game Friday night?"

"I don't know."

"Do you have a functioning brain?"

"I don't know."

I believe the most vulnerable people on the face of the earth are those people who don't know what they believe. I'm not talking about people who are in the process of forming their beliefs; I'm talking about those who are too lazy to think things through and form an opinion, or who just don't care.

When it comes to their faith, many teenagers don't even know that they don't know what they believe. They can repeat what they've heard their parents or Sunday school teachers say, but they have no foundation for making that belief their own.

So how *do* you discover what you believe, and how do you build on that belief to establish the kind of foundation you can live by?

> *Many teenagers don't even know*
> *that they don't know*
> *what they believe.*

Who Cares?

Why is it important to know what you believe?

Because what you believe will determine how you live. What you believe affects your behavior.

Picture this. You're walking in the forest at night and a big black dog crosses the path in front of you. It is so dark that you can't make out what it is. All you know is that something black moved. Your whole body gets involved here. Your eyeballs immediately send a message to your brain: "It's a bear." Your feet do not argue with your eyeballs. They burn a hole in the ground getting you out of there. It doesn't matter whether you saw a shadow or a piece of cardboard or a rock. If you *believe* it's a bear, your body will respond just as if a bear were really there.

When my first daughter, Traci, was a toddler, I put her into the bathtub and forgot she was there. Forty-five minutes later, I was reading the newspaper when I heard her scream. I ran to the bathroom—and discovered that she had locked the door. Standing outside the door, listening to her screams of terror, I was convinced that she had pulled an electrical appliance into the tub and was electrocuting herself. I broke down my bathroom door to save her life. As I stumbled into the room with pieces of bathroom door hanging from me, she leaned from the tub and showed me her tiny hand, all wrinkled from being in the water. "I'm ruined," she sobbed. It took me an hour to convince her she was not going to spend the rest of her life looking like a prune. What she believed had affected her behavior.

What you believe about God will affect how you live. If you don't know what you believe, you will live an unsure and tentative Christian life. You will be easy prey for those who would like to destroy your faith. Do you really know what you believe, or are you just riding the coattails of your parents' faith? Over the years, I have heard hundreds of students talk about a faith that was not really theirs. They were only repeating what they had heard others say; they had no solid foundation for their own beliefs. There is only one way to get that foundation, and that is to know what you believe and why. The Bible says that you should always be ready to give a reason for your faith.

> But in your hearts set apart Christ as Lord. Always be prepared to give an answer to everyone who asks you to give the reason for the hope that you have. But do this with gentleness and respect. *1 Peter 3:15*

You need this foundation—you need it as much for your own spiritual strength as you need it as a preparation for witnessing to others. When someone asks you why you believe what you do, it isn't enough to say, "Well, that's what my Sunday school teacher told me." Your weak answer won't convince the person you're talking to of anything, and you'll also find yourself wondering whether you really believe it yourself. You can't just bury your head in the ground and hope what you believe is right. If you refuse to investigate the foundation of your faith, then your belief is reduced to an opinion, and opinions are weak foundations for something as important as faith.

As a boy, I was part of a Sunday school class that had eight students. All eight of us belonged to the youth group and took part in the activities of the church. Each of us had at one time given testimony to our faith in front of the church congregation. Yet today, only two of the eight claim any relationship with Christ.

What happened? What causes someone who was enthusiastic about God to suddenly dump the whole thing? One explanation is that they knew what they believed, but then at some time in their lives discovered that what they believed was wrong. Another possibility is that they didn't really know what they believed to start with. Either way, if there's no foundation to your faith, it crumbles as soon as it's challenged. I respect those who know why they *disbelieve* in Christianity more than those who are too lazy to find out why they believe in it. And I have a profound respect for Christians who have taken the time to discover the solid foundation of their faith.

Believing in Christ is not some wimpy cop-out to avoid facing the real world. Those who have discovered the solid evidence for Christianity know that they don't need to be ashamed to express their faith to anyone. The apostle Paul knew exactly what he believed and why. He could say with confidence,

> I am not ashamed of the gospel, because it is the power
> of God for the salvation of everyone who believes.
> *Romans 1:16*

Here are some suggestions to help you know what you believe and why you believe it.

Don't Be Afraid to Ask Questions

Many teenagers (and many adults) are afraid to ask questions or express doubts because they think that it's a sin or that it demonstrates weakness. That's just not true.

This year I started a project to read through the Bible in one year. The margins of my Bible are filled with question marks that represent passages I don't understand. My plan is to come back later and study those passages to discover the answers to these questions. And they're hard questions—but if I leave them unanswered, my faith will be weaker than if I search for the answers.

Another reason kids are reluctant to ask hard questions is that—sad to say—those questions have seldom been well received. Not long ago, I heard a Sunday school teacher scold a child for asking if Jesus ever went to the bathroom. "It's not nice to ask those kinds of questions," he growled.

After the class, I talked to the little boy. I told him that Jesus went to the bathroom just like he and I did. His eyes got very big as he gulped and asked, "Then did Jesus have parts just like we have?"

Okay, I admit it—he surprised me. But I answered, "Yes, he had parts just like us."

"Good," the little boy said, with a relieved sigh, "then I guess he knows how little kids feel." The boy walked away and left me with my mouth hanging open. Just because someone was willing to answer his question, he had come to an excellent if simple theological conclusion: God knows how we feel because he became one of us.

> Since the children have flesh and blood, he too shared in their humanity so that by his death he might destroy him who holds the power of death—that is, the devil—and free those who all their lives were held in slavery by their fear of death.... For this reason he had to be made like his brothers in every way, in order that he might become a merciful and faithful high priest in service to God, and that he might make atonement for the sins of the people. Because he himself suffered when he was tempted, he is able to help those who are being tempted.... For we do not have a high priest who is unable to sympathize with our weaknesses, but we have one who has been tempted in every way, just as we are—yet was without sin. Let us then approach the throne of

grace with confidence, so that we may receive mercy and find grace to help us in our time of need.

Hebrews 2:14–15, 17–18; 4:15–16

Just like the little boy, I had wondered many times whether Jesus could really know how I felt, but it wasn't until I had the courage to ask the question that someone showed me the above Scripture. I had hesitated to ask because it sounded so irreverent—and, like the little guy I told you about, I had been scolded more than once for asking the wrong question. But it *wasn't* irreverent. It was an honest question, and I'm so glad it has been answered.

Don't be afraid to ask, and to keep on asking until you get some answers. And don't settle for just another opinion—make sure the answers are anchored in truth from the Word of God.

And that leads to the second suggestion.

Learn to Study the Scriptures to Know Why You Believe

From time to time, there have been intelligent people—C. S. Lewis, Frank Morison, and Josh McDowell are good examples—who set out to disprove the Christian faith. They were filled with doubts and questions that they believed would destroy the logical foundation of Christianity. But in their aggressive pursuit of the truth, they found answers to their questions, and those answers convinced them that Christ really was Lord. Rather than disproving Christianity, they became believers. They found those answers in the Bible.

The one element that keeps what you believe from being just another opinion is the Scriptures. They are the bedrock foundation from which you can discover who God is and what he wants with your life.

Know What You Believe

In 1989 a powerful earthquake hit San Francisco, California. Most of the buildings in the city had very little damage because they had been built on solid foundations. Those that were destroyed had been built on landfill. When the earthquake hit, those weak foundations of loose dirt turned to jelly, and the walls came tumbling down. If your faith is built on hearsay and opinion, it's like a building without a solid foundation. It may look strong on the outside, but it will never hold up under pressure—which is just when you need it most.

Comedian and speaker Pat Hurley asked several thousand students at a youth gathering if they believed that God loved them. A roar of enthusiastic approval went up from the crowd. *Of course* they believed that God loved them. Then he asked if anyone in the audience could quote a Bible verse other than John 3:16 that said that God loved them. In that huge crowd of wonderful kids, only one boy knew of such a verse. You may say, "So what?" But when one of those teenagers faces tragedy or heartbreak and needs to know for sure that God still cares, the memory of that whooping crowd will not help. When the earthquakes of life strike, just remembering that someone told you God loves you won't be enough. In times like those, your faith will stand only if it is built on the solid rock of God's Word.

The greatest single thing you can do to strengthen your faith is to get hooked on God's Word.

Want to give it a try? Then here's a list of suggestions that will help you search the Word of God for what you believe.

1. *Come to the Bible with an open heart.*

If the Bible really is God's Word to us, then it's important not to twist its meaning. Too often we read the

Know What You Believe

Bible to find evidence for something we already believe, to seek support for something someone has told us, or to make it say what we want it to say. Instead, approach the Bible with an open heart, ready to receive whatever it says—even if what it says contradicts your opinions or preconceived ideas. I admit it: There have been many times I have gone to the Bible to prove that I was right about something, only to discover I was wrong.

By taking verses out of context and by twisting meanings, you can misuse the Bible to support almost anything. Racists misuse it to back up their hatred, for example, and people hungry for power use it to make people submit to them. It can be misused by you and me as well, unintentionally as well as intentionally. Don't fall into that trap—read the Bible to find out what it says, not to make it mean whatever you want.

2. *As you study the Bible, pray.*

Pray that God will give you the open heart I discussed above, and that you will be willing to accept the truth he reveals. Ask God to take away any ulterior motives and to give you a heart hungry for his truth and the courage to apply it in your life.

3. *Use the Bible as your primary source of truth.*

As vital as it is to read Christian material and to listen to pastors, youth workers, and other men and women of God, it is also essential that you weigh what they say against the Bible. Many of God's people have been led astray because they chose to believe the messenger rather than the one who gave the message. The more you read the Bible, the less chance there is of being misled.

> I am astonished that you are so quickly deserting the
> one who called you by the grace of Christ and are
> turning to a different gospel—which is really no gospel at

all. Evidently some people are throwing you into confusion and are trying to pervert the gospel of Christ. But even if we or an angel from heaven should preach a gospel other than the one we preached to you, let him be eternally condemned! As we have already said, so now I say again: If anybody is preaching to you a gospel other than what you accepted, let him be eternally condemned! Am I now trying to win the approval of men, or of God? Or am I trying to please men? If I were still trying to please men, I would not be a servant of Christ. I want you to know, brothers, that the gospel I preached is not something that man made up.   *Galatians 1:6–11*

4. *Study the Bible as a whole.*

Choosing a word or sentence from the Bible without considering the entire context is like trying to catch the meaning of a conversation by hearing just a few words. The authors of the Bible wrote each book with a purpose. When you understand that purpose and know something about the people they were writing to, it's much easier to understand individual passages. Any single passage must be considered in the context of the rest of the book of the Bible that it appears in, the purpose of that book, and the message of the Bible as a whole.

"Wait," you may be saying, "I don't know all of that stuff! And I don't have time to learn it all—I just have a few minutes a day to read the Bible. Now I'll never understand it." Don't get discouraged. There are some things to remember:

First, there are lots of helpful resources to let you see what you are studying in context. Some of them even explain how cultural practices of biblical times affect the meaning of what you're reading.   Here are some of the better resources.

Understanding Scripture by Alvera M. Michelsen and A. Berkley Michelsen, Regal, 1982.

A Layman's Guide to Interpreting the Bible by Walter A.

Henrichsen, Zondervan Publishing House, 1985.

The NIV Student Bible, New International Version, 1989, Zondervan Bible Publishers, shows four different ways to read completely through the Bible.

Life Application Bible by Tyndale House Publishers, Inc. and Youth for Christ/USA, 1988, has excellent introductions to each chapter, context notes, and ideas for application.

Serendipity Bible, Zondervan Publishing House, 1988.

And second, remember that studying the Bible is a continuing process. Don't feel bad that you don't know as much right now as you would like to know. Many who have spent their lives studying the Scripture feel the same way. But the more you study, the more you know, and the more you know, the easier it is to understand. Don't let your lack of knowledge keep you from digging in. Your understanding of God and the strength of your faith will grow as you continue. You aren't alone—the Holy Spirit is also working to help you understand what you're reading. He's your partner every time you sit down to study.

5. *Make use of other Christian resources.*

The Christian bookstore is rich with resources that can strengthen your faith and help you know what you believe. If this book is helpful to you, then be aware that there are thousands of others that can help you in a variety of ways. If you wanted to know how to cure polio, it would be silly to start from scratch and not take advantage of all the research that has gone on before. Likewise, you can take advantage of those who have struggled with some of the same questions you have —always keeping in mind, of course, that the Bible is your primary source of truth. No matter how famous or respected the author, what you read in that writer's books must always be weighed against the standard of the Bible.

Here are some excellent books to start with:

Know What You Believe by Paul Little, InterVarsity Press, 1985, is one of the best books on this subject. It is short and easy to read.

Reason to Believe by R. C. Sproul, Zondervan Publishing House, 1982, is an excellent book that gives responses to some of the objections people have to Christianity. This is a book that will help you know the answers to some of the hard questions your friends and you may have.

Know the Truth by Bruce Milne, InterVarsity Press, 1982, and *Evidence That Demands a Verdict*, by Josh McDowell, Campus Crusade, 1981, are excellent books that cover the subject of belief in detail. They are not easy to read because they deal with the very deepest and most difficult issues of the faith, but they are well worth it. For the motivated student who really wants some in-depth answers they are a must.

All of these books, plus the Bible study aids I mentioned before them, can be purchased at most Christian bookstores. If they don't have them in stock, they'll be happy to order them for you. If you want to really discover the strength of your faith, get those books and set out to find answers to questions like these:

What sets Christianity apart from any other religions in the world?

How do I know that what the Bible says is true?

What do I say to those who claim that it doesn't matter what I believe as long as I'm sincere?

What evidence is there that Jesus really was God?

Is there any proof that Jesus rose from the dead?

And here's another suggestion: Catechism or

confirmation classes are also great places to pick up a lot of the basic information on Christianity. I admit it—on the surface, those classes aren't always the most exciting places to be. But the material you'll study there is the stuff upon which the faith is built. When your faith in Christ is under attack by a teacher or a friend or by your own doubts, the beliefs taught in these classes are what you'll need to fight off that attack. Like the strong foundation of a building, those beliefs are the foundation that has allowed our faith to stand through hundreds of years of adversity.

And don't attend those classes just to please your parents or to get by. Try to *understand* what you are being taught—and *ask questions!*

Bet Your Life on It

Put what you believe to the test. It's when you really see God work in your own life that the final unshakable touches of strength are added to what you believe.

In college, I was given an assignment to teach a class as creatively as possible. I taught the law of the pendulum, a law of physics that states that a pendulum can never return to a point higher than the point from which it is released. If you put a ball on the end of a string and release it so that it is free to swing, when it returns it can't go any higher than the point from which you released it. In fact, because of friction and gravity, it will fall short of the release point. Each time it swings, the arc gets smaller and smaller until it finally comes to rest. I used all kinds of diagrams, mathematical formulas, and models to teach the law of the pendulum to the class, and I could tell by the look on the teacher's face that he thought I had done well.

When I finished, I asked the class how many believed

in the law of the pendulum. All hands flew up, including the teacher's. He thought the lesson was over—but it had just started. I asked him to come to the front of the room and sit in a chair placed against the wall. Suspended from the ceiling was 250 pounds of weight-lifting disks. This was a *big* pendulum. I brought the 250 pounds of metal right up to his nose and said, "If the law of the pendulum is true, then when I release this mass of metal, it will swing across the room and return short of where I am holding it now. Your nose will still look like it does right now." I looked him right in the eye and said, "Sir, do you believe this law is true?"

There was a long pause as great drops of sweat formed on his upper lip. Then, weakly, he nodded and whispered, "Yes."

I released the pendulum. At the far end of its arc it paused momentarily and then started back. I have never seen a man move so fast in my life!

Carefully, I stepped around the still-swinging pendulum and asked the class, "Does he believe in the law of the pendulum?"

In unison they answered, "No!"

My professor *understood* the law, but he was unwilling to trust his nose to it. After a short discussion, a student volunteered to sit in the chair. Even though his face contorted in fear as the pendulum started back, he stayed put. But it stopped an inch from his nose and swung away from him again. Now his faith in that law was strengthened. The next time the pendulum swung, he didn't even blink.

When you go beyond just knowing about God and begin to trust him with your life, that's when you really know what you believe. As you study the Bible and discover principles that God endorses, put them into practice in your life. It's risky business; it's not always easy to obey God in this way. But when you trust your nose to what you say you believe and discover that he is faithful, your faith will be strengthened.

And there's no better time to do that than right now.

CHAPTER
4

GETTING
ALONG WITH
YOUR PARENTS

After I delivered a great speech on how families could learn to love each other, a young girl came up to me. "Oh, Mr. Davis," she gushed, "I wish you were my dad." So there I stood, feeling like a pretty successful father—until I heard a strange noise and looked over my shoulder to see my thirteen-year-old daughter sticking her finger in her throat and making gagging noises.

Because I had made a nice speech, the little girl in the audience thought I was the perfect father. But my daughter, who has to live with me every day, knew the truth.

One of the skills that will serve you best in life is the skill of getting along with other people. The best place to learn that skill is in your own home. It always seems easier to get along with other people than the ones you love the most. That's because you have to *live* with the people you love. You know their weaknesses and they know yours. And all of those weaknesses are amplified when you live with each other.

This chapter will give you some hints on how to get along with your parents. If you want the full treatment of this subject, I recommend a book by one of the finest authors who has ever lived. The book is titled *How to Live with Your Parents Without Losing Your Mind*. I am the author—and don't you dare stick your finger down your throat and make any disgusting noises.

The three suggestions I'm going to make in this chapter are:

1. *Give your parents the right to be wrong.*
2. *Believe that they really love you.*
3. *Learn how to show them love.*

Give Your Parents the Right to Be Wrong

Parents don't get the chance to *practice* being parents.

Parenting is something they just try to do the best they can.

Maybe it would be a good idea for parents to borrow someone else's kid for a few years before they have their own. That way, they could learn without damaging the lives of their own children. Unfortunately, not many families are willing to offer their children for such an experiment. Parents have to learn to parent using their own children, so *you* are the guinea pig.

"Wait," you say, "I have three older brothers and sisters. How come Mom and Dad couldn't have perfected their technique on them?" Because you are totally different from your brothers and sisters, so you require a special touch. Parenting isn't easy even if you have five kids.

Before my daughters were born I taught adults how to raise children, but that still didn't prepare me for the real thing. In fact, I wish I could go back and apologize to all those people for some of the things I said. At that time in my life I didn't even *want* to have children. It wasn't that I disliked kids—it was just that I had met a child once, and it was not pleasant.

I had been invited to dinner at the home of some friends, and they sat me next to their one-and-a-half-year-old baby. That was one of the grossest experiences in all my life. That child smeared food all over his body and hid about two hundred peas in his left ear. He smeared Jello all over himself and then he got friendly with me.

On the way home, I told my wife I never wanted to have children. The doctors told us we probably couldn't have kids anyway—but God had something different in mind. On May 9, 1975, Traci Davis was born, and three years later her sister Taryn came to fight with her. Even though I didn't want to have children, the moment those girls were born I was consumed with love for them. I wanted to be the best dad in

I Don't Remember Dropping the Skunk, But . . .   54

the whole world. But because I am human, I've made many mistakes along the way. I once accused Traci of lying when she was telling the truth. I have said no when I should have said yes. At times I have been too busy to listen when they wanted to talk to me. Sometimes I have been too strict—not because I don't love them, but because I'm afraid that something bad might happen to them, and I want to protect them from it. And, yes, I have expected them to be perfect, even though I'm not. I love them more now than when they were born—but despite that love, I still make mistakes.

A few weeks ago, I was away from home and Traci called me to ask if she could go to a party. Because the party was being held at an adult nightclub, I said no. She was so disappointed that, as she explained how important this party was to her, she began to cry. She reminded me of my promise to give her more privileges as she grew older. "I'm older *now*," she cried, "and still you don't trust me!"

I tried to explain that, although I *did* trust her, I was uncomfortable with this particular situation. As she continued to cry, my heart was breaking—I wanted so much to say yes and make her happy, but I held my ground. I told her that I loved her very much and wanted her to be happy, but I had to make a judgment call. I promised that, together, we would look for other opportunities where she could have some of that freedom that she so desperately wanted. We set a time to talk about it further.

As I hung up the phone, I was filled with self doubt. After all, I couldn't be *absolutely sure* I was right. I just hoped that she knew I was trying my best to be a good dad.

We had that talk a few days later, and it turned out to be one of the best we'd ever had. I agreed to allow her to argue her case and to disagree with me, and I agreed to be more

Getting Along with Your Parents

sensitive to her needs. Although she didn't completely agree with my reasoning, she accepted the fact that I have the responsibility to make those difficult decisions, and she agreed to forgive me when she thinks I might be wrong.

Admitting that I'm wrong is hard for me—I'm afraid it will make me look like a weak parent. You may discover that your parents won't admit their mistakes for the same reason. They feel it may erode their authority. Those are probably the times that it's hardest for you to forgive them, because it seems they're just stacking one wrong on top of another. And let's face it—if you're a normal human being, you also find it difficult to admit that you're wrong. Yet you want to be forgiven for those mistakes. Why not give your parents the same forgiveness? If you do, it will be a giant step toward a better relationship with them.

Believe That They Love You

Most teenagers have a sneaking suspicion that the first thought that crosses their parents' minds when they get up in the morning is, "How can I make my children suffer today?" That just isn't true. Although sometimes the decisions made by your parents cause you unhappiness, 99% of the time their motive is just the opposite. They believe that the unhappiness caused by their decision is outweighed by the sorrow they are trying to save you.

Your parents' fear for your safety may cause them to overreact at times. Does this story sound familiar? On a Saturday night, you come home twenty minutes later than your curfew. When you open the door, your father and mother are waiting for you. The veins in your father's neck are bigger than your legs. With eyes glaring and spit flying, he tells you how inconsiderate you have been and then announces that you are grounded for fifty years. You run to your room crying that he doesn't understand. As you lie in bed, you decide that he probably waited up all evening just to ruin your life.

Now let me tell you what really happened inside your dad's head. If he's anything like me, he loves you very much, and because of that he was worried before you even left. After all, think of the terrible things that *could* happen.

Your dad's fear kicked into high gear the first minute you were late. In the book *How to Live with Your Parents Without Losing Your Mind,* I talk about the worry gremlin that lives inside your parent's heads. As soon as you're late, this little monster goes to his files and brings out the most terrible things that could happen to you. Many of them are ridiculous or impossible, but the gremlin doesn't care. They don't have to be possible—they just have to be terrible. He puts those ideas into your parents' minds. Five minutes after your curfew, he has convinced your father that you have been in a terrible auto accident, or that you have been trampled by a herd of wild shoppers at a K-Mart blue-light special.

Fifteen minutes after your curfew, your dad is ready to call the police. His stomach is in knots and he's burping a lot. If the telephone rings, he'll jump—he's sure the morgue is calling for him to come identify your body.

Approaching twenty minutes past curfew, he's sure you're dead. Tears are forming as he gets ready to initiate a national search for your mutilated body.

And at that moment you open the door, and he screams, "I'm going to kill you!"

Is he right to yell at you so harshly? Is he right to assume that you don't care about anybody but yourself? Probably not. But perhaps you can better understand his momentary loss of sanity if you know that love and fear caused the explosion. Exploding is easier than admitting that he was frightened to death that something terrible had happened. His real feelings would be more appropriately expressed by holding you in his arms and telling you about the stampede at K-Mart, but because it is hard for a parent to admit those kind of fears, he yells instead.

Can you forgive him for that? Can you see through his anger to the simple fact that he cares? If you can, then you can also see how important it is to get home on time. If you believe your parents love you and realize how unreasonably fearful they can be, it should motivate you to reduce that fear whenever you can. If you're going to be late, call to let them know.

After youth group the other night, the people who were bringing Traci home decided to stop for ice cream. The phone rang about five minutes before she was due to be home. She asked if she could go for some ice cream and told me when she expected to be home. The worry gremlin never came out that night. Because of her consideration, the only thought I gave to her being out late was that I hoped she had a good time.

It's easy to misinterpret your parents' interest in where you are and who you're with as a lack of trust. It's probably not a lack of trust—it's simply an overdose of love. You'll find Mom and Dad a lot less stressful if you take the time to let them know where you're going and who you'll be with. If your plans change, let them know. More than one manhunt for a perfectly safe teenager has been started because the teenager changed his mind and went somewhere else without letting his parents know.

The first day I dropped Traci off at junior high, I was tempted to put her in a different school. There were kids coming out of that building with hairstyles you could be injured on. Everything looked so big and dangerous. I loved her so much that I thought I should protect her from all this. Of course, if I had tried to do what I was tempted to do, she would have disowned me forever. But I was tempted to do it anyway—not because I wanted to make her miserable, but because I loved her so much.

Why is it so important to believe that your parents love you? Because otherwise, you will always think of them as your enemy. If you're constantly second-guessing their motives, you'll have a much harder time responding to them in a civil manner. And what you believe about them is also what you'll expect from them. Even when you disobey, you still love your parents and want them to believe that. As a dad who cares deeply for his daughters and yet makes occasional decisions that cause them to wonder about that, please believe me—your parents do love you.

Respond to Them in Love

It would be easy for you to quit at this point.

I've challenged you to allow your parents the right to be wrong, and you can easily respond, "Yup, my parents are weird—but I'll forgive them."

I've challenged you to believe that your parents love you, and you might even agree that they love you and just have a strange way of showing it.

But if you're really going to make headway in getting along with your parents, you must take the final and most difficult step: Show them you love them.

Unfortunately, many teenagers spend much of their lives responding negatively to their parents. I spent eighteen years living with my family, and I can't remember a single moment when I tried to make my home a better place for the other people who lived there. My number-one concern was to get as much as I could for me.

Just before he was crucified, Jesus told his disciples that, to let other people know they were his followers, they should love each other in the same way that he loved them (John 13:35). Similarly, your demonstration of Christ's love toward the other members of your family will be the most powerful influence on changing your home. In *How to Live with Your Parents Without Losing Your Mind,* I stated over and over again that you can do nothing to change the behavior of your parents—but you can do everything to change your own attitude and behavior toward them. When Jesus told his disciples to love each other, he was not talking about a feeling; he was talking about action. The question is not, Why should I love my parents? The question is, *How* can I love my parents?

Let me suggest two answers: First, love them with your words—and second, love them with your actions.

Say the Magic Words

On my dad's sixtieth birthday, I sent him a birthday card with a picture of an ugly cowboy on the front. Inside was some funny saying both of us have forgotten. Next to that saying I wrote six simple words: "Happy Birthday Dad, I love you."

My dad called me the day the card arrived. With emotion in his voice, he thanked me for remembering his birthday. Most of all he thanked me for writing "I love you." He said he couldn't remember any time I had ever said that to him before. My first reaction was defensive. I was sure I *had* said it before, and I was ready to argue that I couldn't remember the last time he had said it to me either.

Then it hit me. It didn't matter how long it had been since he had told me. Love isn't something you keep score for. "I've given you fifteen loves, and you've only given me three!" How silly! If Jesus had kept score, we'd have lost the game of life before it even started. My dad was right—I had been very selfish with my expression of love. I couldn't remember ever saying it to him. Today things are different—in fact, as I wrote this (on a plane), I was reminded again that it has been too long since I have said those words. When the plane landed, I called to say it one more time.

When was the last time you said those words to your mom and dad? After a three-day conference where dozens of teenagers made serious commitments to follow Christ, I encouraged them to call home. I suggested that the best way to show their newfound faith was to call their parents and tell them how much they loved them. With the exception of a few parents who were insensitive and suspicious (probably because they had never heard anything like this before), the results were astounding. Some parents had not heard those wonderful words for a long time, and for many it was the beginning of new communication.

In the Bible, God continually reminds us of his love. Without those reminders, the Christian life would be pretty discouraging. Take the time to say those magic words to the people in your family.

Do the Magic Words

As beautiful as it is that God cared enough to tell us of his love, ultimately it was an *act* of love that changed the world forever. God didn't just stay up in heaven sending us love notes —he sent his only Son Jesus Christ to die on the cross, forever proving his love.

How should you show love to your parents? Should you hug them when you say it, or plant slobbery kisses like your aunt always bestows on you when she sees you? Although these are important expressions of love, the kind that changes lives goes further. The kind of love I'm talking about is expressed in the little things, but it affects the lives of others in a big way.

Getting Along with Your Parents

For example, keeping your room clean is one of the greatest expressions of love you can show to your mom. "WHAT?" you say. "Give me something else. I'll hug everybody in my house fifty times a day, but why should I keep my room clean?" The answer is simple: It makes your mother very happy. You would not believe the tension that would be relieved in your home if you would do just two things—help with household chores without being asked, and keep your own room clean. The effort it takes is not very much compared to the grief it avoids.

It's hard to believe that the love of God can be expressed in such simple things. Yet that is exactly how love is expressed in all aspects of life. If Christianity is so limited to singing and talking about something that we never do anything about it in real life, then it doesn't apply to real life, does it? Jesus didn't just talk about love—he showed it.

How you live at home has a big effect on how you will live when you leave. Don't be deceived into thinking that when you leave home, you'll leave behind all the problems you had getting along with those people. It's just not true. You'll carry the same attitudes you developed at home into your relationships with other people.

So please—give your parents a break. Allow them to make some mistakes, believe that they love you, and respond to them with the kind of love that can only come by trusting Christ for the ability to do it.

Then you—and your family, too—will be able to see what a difference love makes.

CHAPTER 5

LOOKING FOR SOMEONE TO LOVE

I was walking down the hall between classes when I saw her. I had gone to school with Becky for eight years, but this was the first time I'd *really* seen her. At that moment, there was nothing more beautiful on the face of the earth. Her long eyelashes cooled the air as she blinked, and oh, those eyes.

Why was I feeling this way? She had looked right at me with those same eyes only a few days ago, and it hadn't bothered me then. Why was my heart beating so fast now? Speaking of my heart, I thought it was going to come right out of my chest. I wondered if she could see my shirt flopping around from its pounding. And what if it came right out? How embarrassing to be standing in the hall with my heart flopping around on the floor. Everybody would be laughing—but worst of all, *she* would be standing there watching me try to catch it and put it back in. I would never be able to look her in the face again.

She was closer now, and I wasn't sure I would survive. Just as she passed, she turned to her friend and smiled. The light reflecting off her lip gloss almost blinded me. Then she was gone. Only the lingering fragrance of her perfume remained. Knees shaking, I leaned against the wall.

It seems like it happens over night. One night you go to bed dreaming of catching snakes, climbing trees, playing with toys, and jumping rope. The next morning you wake up and they are everywhere. The world has been invaded by the O.S. (opposite sex). You knew they were there all along, but you never really noticed before. What had been a nuisance now looks pretty nice. All kinds of wonderful squirrelly feelings invade your body, and you seem to spend all your time thinking about the O.S. They're in your mind, on the phone, at school, all over the beach, *everywhere*.

The whole thing is part of God's plan. It's the beginning

of the very natural process of finding someone to share life with. Those first weird feelings are the sparks that will eventually light the fire of true love. The decisions you make during this important time in your life *can* make this one of the most exciting and happy times of your life. But *wrong* decisions at this important time can make you feel miserable now and can lead to sorrow and heartbreak in the future.

The information in this chapter can help you enjoy this part of your life and will also give you some guidelines for a better chance of establishing a successful and fulfilling marriage.

Many authors might title this chapter "Dating." But I think dating is only *part* of the process of looking for someone to love. The process begins with your first interest in the O.S. and continues through several stages until marriage. The stages are: casual friendships, dating, serious dating, engagement, and marriage.

God is interested in your love life. Yet of all the areas of your life, that is definitely one of the hardest to give to him. It's easy to trust God with what you do on Sunday, but to trust him with prom dates, boyfriends, girlfriends, and steadies? That's a different story. One of the reasons for our reluctance is that we don't really believe God has our best interests at heart. I was afraid that God wanted me to marry someone I wasn't attracted to and who would show no interest in sex. I was afraid that when I finally trusted him, he would open a curtain to reveal this hideous creature that I was supposed to spend the rest of my life with.

We don't *trust* God—and that's ironic, because this is an area of our life that God especially wants to bless. He wants you to have a fulfilling love life; he wants to help you avoid some of the devastating pitfalls that await the unsuspecting teenager who may try to navigate these waters alone.

Are you willing to seek God's guidance and follow his guidelines as you develop relationships with the O.S.? Committing that part of your life to him is the first step—and it's the most important step you can take.

Friendships

When that first surge of adrenalin courses through your body at the sight of the O.S., you might want to jump right into the hunt. That's why a lot of teenagers start out their love life with some pretty serious dating. I want to suggest a different approach: Use your teenage years to develop as many friends of the opposite sex as you can.

It's easy to immediately focus on the first good-looking guy or girl who crosses your path and forget about the other opportunities for friendship that surround you. Sure, there are some very successful marriages that began with a single relationship early in high school (or even junior high), but they're the exception rather than the rule. Most of the people in such marriages feel cheated that they weren't able to date and have friendships with more people. Don't make that mistake; take this opportunity to develop many friends.

The experience of developing many friendships will give you a strong foundation on which to build more serious relationships later. It will also allow you to see a wider variety of partners from which to choose. You may even develop friendships that will last a lifetime. There are many adults who have never really had a true friend of the opposite sex. And, unfortunately, many marriages are between people who have never really been friends.

Casual Dating

After my knees stopped shaking, I made my way to

class. But I couldn't get Becky out of my mind. If only those beautiful eyes would look directly into mine so she could see how I felt.

Suddenly I could smell her perfume again. She was in a different room, but by some miracle the air conditioning system was bringing her perfume to me.

Then I heard her gently call my name—"Ken." The next time her voice seemed harsher: "Ken!"

I snapped out of my daydream and looked up into the face of Mr. Brooks, my history teacher. It was obvious from the laughter of the class that he had asked me a question. I didn't know what he had asked, but since we had been studying recent political history I ventured a guess at the answer. I don't remember much that I learned in high school, but the outburst of hysteria that followed my answer has burned into my mind forever that Richard Nixon was not the first woman to run for vice-president of the United States.

After class, I found Gary Ripple, the most experienced boy I knew. I didn't know the first thing about dating, and I thought he could help me know how to approach Becky. Gary told me that, first, I should call her and ask her out. Then he told me how to go to her house and meet her terrifying parents. He gave me careful instructions on how to walk her to the car, open her door, and let her in, then walk around to the driver's side and let myself in. I'm glad he went into such detail. I probably would have opened her door and then crawled over her to get to the driver's side.

"When you come home," he said, "you just do everything in reverse. Get out of your side of the car, then go around and open her door and let her out. Say, 'I had a very nice evening. I hope we can do this again sometime,' then kiss her and leave."

I had kissed dozens of mirrors in my life, but never a girl. Just the thought of it sent cold chills up my spine. I went home and practiced. I would dress up and practice my lines over the phone with the dial tone buzzing in my ear. I would walk my collie, Ralph, to the car, open the door, and let him in. I was always careful not to slam his tail in the door. I'm sure there were some people in our neighborhood who thought I was dating a real dog. I would drive Ralph around and then come home, reverse the whole process, and walk Ralph back to the house. No—I did not kiss Ralph. But to this day whenever I see a collie, I can smell Becky's perfume.

And this, friends, is the second stage in looking for love. And I'm not talking about dating dogs. I'm talking about casual dating—spending time with special friends of the O.S. without getting too involved.

Keep It Light

You started out with a large circle of friendships, many of them with people of the opposite sex. Now, you find that there are some of them you would like to get to know better, or maybe some who have indicated that they want to get to know you better. The key is to *keep it light*. Hold back on the emotional and physical involvement so that you can take the time to get to know some of the more interesting people you have met.

Serious physical and emotional involvement gets in the way of getting to know someone. I have talked with hundreds of teenagers who have been involved with a boy or girl for months, even years, and yet know very little about the person they've been dating. They know what turns each other on, what makes each other jealous, and what kind of hamburger to order, but they have no idea what dreams their partner has

Looking for Someone to Love

for the future, what relationship they have with the Lord, or what brings them real joy, sorrow, or fear. It seems odd, but casual dating is the stage at which you begin to really know someone, to talk openly and honestly about the things that are really important to you. Bypassing that stage might result in being seriously involved with someone you hardly know.

In casual dating, you shouldn't have to worry about a wrestling match in the back seat, or foggy windows overlooking some beautiful scenic spot that you can't see anyway. Do I sound like a prude? Maybe it's just because I've talked to so many kids who have been disappointed because every relationship started with intense physical and emotional involvement and never got any further. So casual dating should be just that: casual, fun, and free from the stress that comes when you get more involved.

If you find it hard to avoid getting tangled up at this stage of the game, choose locations and activities that will take some of that pressure away. For instance: If you choose the right people to go with you, dating with other couples is often less stressful, more fun, and takes some of the sexual tension out of a date. If you're dating alone and you prefer to keep things light, go where there will be lots of other people. It's much easier to keep it light if you avoid long periods of time in parked cars and dark corners.

Understand the Meaning of Love

It's important, as you begin dating, to understand the meaning of love, because at this stage you may begin to experience feelings that go beyond just friendship. Right up front, let me say that those feelings are natural and okay—but feeling them is not reason enough to dive headfirst into a full-blown serious relationship.

Don't confuse sexual and physical attraction or romantic feelings with love. Many marriages are on the rocks today because someone assumed that love is that wonderful fireworks feeling you get when you are with the right person. The tingling excitement that accompanies a kiss, and the increased pulse rate when that special person walks into the room—those are wonderful feelings, but they aren't necessarily love. Shortly after marriage, those feelings diminish. But they're replaced with something even better: a deeper kind of love. If the definition of love is limited to those feelings, it would be easy to assume that because the intense feelings are gone, love is gone.

I've been married to the same woman for twenty years. If my heart had continued to flutter every time she entered the room, I'd have died of a heart attack years ago. But I love her a million times more today than I did when my heart danced every time I saw her.

I'm not trying to diminish the importance of those special emotions. They were invented by God himself to get the fire going. But they're *not to be confused with love*. When an exceptionally beautiful woman walks by, or when I meet someone who is extremely fascinating, my heart still starts beating faster. Does that mean I'm no longer in love with my wife? Does it mean I'm in love with this new person? No way —it means I still have blood running through my veins and have the ability to recognize beauty when I see it.

I have friends who have confused romance with love —and have paid a very dear price for their mistake. The excitement of meeting a new and attractive person led one friend to assume that, because those feelings didn't exist with his wife of fifteen years, he didn't love her anymore. So he left

Looking for Someone to Love

his wife to begin a new, more exciting relationship.

His marriage to his new partner lasted one year. As soon as the newness wore off, so did the romantic excitement. Then my friend realized his mistake. But it was too late.

Don't place too much importance on the thrill of romance. Enjoy it, but please don't let it be your main reason for getting serious about someone—and *for sure* don't let it be your main reason for choosing a mate.

Choose the One to Love

The title of this chapter is "Looking for Someone to Love," not "Waiting for Love to Happen to Me." You don't "fall into love," as the old saying implies. You *choose* the one you will love. *Falling* in love implies that, one day, out of the blue, you meet someone—and a naked little cupid shoots you in the rear with an arrow and you suddenly feel all the right goose bumps.

If that's love, then what happens when you wake up one day and *don't* feel that emotion anymore? Have you fallen back out of love? Did the little cupid pull his arrow back out?

There's still a lot of romance in my marriage, but there are also times when I feel anger toward my wife. There are times when my heart rate might have a hard time keeping pace with a turtle. Do I still love her a million times more than when we first met? Yes. And of course there are also many times when she makes my heart beat faster without a naked little cupid within a hundred miles. She's still the only one I want to spend my life with.

Love is a commitment you make to another human. It's not just a gooey feeling.

Of course, romance will be a part of courtship—but use some other criteria as well. Don't just say, "Does this person

give me goose bumps? Yes. Okay, that's all I need to know."
Ask yourself some other questions as well. Questions like
these, for instance:

What do we have in common?

Do we hold the same moral and spiritual values?

Does this person lift me up or pull me down?

Is this a person that I could spend the rest of my life
with?

Choose Carefully

I can hear you screaming already: "Wait a minute, Ken,
I'm not getting married here! I'm just thinking about going
out on a date!"

If you get to the point where you're kissing and
holding each other, if you begin struggling with sexual
temptation, or if you start whispering "I love you," then
you're much closer to marriage than you would ever believe.
Once you get serious, it's all too easy to ignore the danger
signals.

That's why I'm taking the time now to talk about
careful choices. Christians who swore that they would only
marry another believer have ended up in unequal and miserable
marriages because, back when they were casually dating, they
felt it was okay to date someone who didn't love the Lord.
Girls who sensed dangerous tendencies in the boys they were
casually dating have ended up in abusive marriages because
they let their hearts get in front of their heads.

The time to carefully look at the qualities of your
friends, to ask yourself what kind of mate they would make, is
before you get too deeply involved. There is truth to the old
statement, "Love is blind." Once you begin to let your heart
go, it can be too late. You're willing to give your partner the

benefit of an awful lot of doubts, to believe that the power of your love is enough to make your partner change.

It doesn't work that way. Choose even your casual dates carefully.

Serious Dating

The day had finally arrived for the real thing. I had just about worn out the telephone with all my dress rehearsals, and my dog Ralph was starting to get cranky about getting his tail slammed in the car door. I think he was ashamed to be seen riding around with me; he would duck when we met other cars.

So, on a Wednesday night, I picked up the phone and dialed her number. "Hello," a gruff male voice answered. I hung up. Sweat was dripping from my forehead. I waited about thirty minutes and then called again.

This time Becky answered the phone. I don't know what I said to her. It wasn't even close to the speech I had memorized. I remember babbling something about how nice she looked at the drinking fountain and how I wanted to take her bowling Saturday. I'm sure glad she couldn't see me—now I was slobbering as well as sweating.

I have absolutely no recall of what she said, except for the word *yes*. When I heard that, I gurgled a few more words, hung up, and fell to the floor in a pitiful puddle.

On the big night, I made my way to her front door with weak knees. I met the father connected to the gruff voice and made small talk waiting for Becky to come out of the deep recesses of that secret place girls hide as they prepare for a date. I tried to sound mature and responsible, but every five seconds my voice would break from its normal, mellow, manly tone and sound like someone stepped on a mouse.

Finally we were on our way. And, surprisingly, the

night went perfectly—with one minor hitch. I opened the door on her side of the car and said, "Get in Ralph."

When we came home, I was on cloud nine. I quickly got out of the car and opened her door. But my knees turned to rubber as we walked toward the porch—now it was time for the big "K." I was sure the neighbors had their telescopes trained on us and that her brothers and sisters were under the porch watching. Sweating, I launched into my carefully rehearsed speech that would end with the big "K." After three words, I was babbling again, and starting to slobber.

Then she was gone. She had said something very nice, squeezed my hand, and disappeared into the house. I could hear her father's voice inside, and I instinctively knew that it wouldn't be a good idea to barge in and say, "Wait a minute —we didn't do the big 'K' yet."

But even without the big "K," it had been an exciting night. I went home and told Ralph every detail.

That date was a long time ago. It may seem silly to you that I would be so concerned over something as "trivial" as a kiss. To me, because of the incredible feelings I had for Becky and because it was my first "real" date, *every* aspect of that evening was very important.

And, as we discuss serious dating, you'll see that I firmly believe that kisses are not trivial. No part of exploring the possibility of a lifelong relationship with someone is trivial. I think that teenagers should have dozens of relationships with the O.S. where kissing isn't even an issue. Serious dating—that exciting world where kissing *is* an issue—is where you begin to unleash your heart. It should be done only with qualified people, and on a much more limited basis.

What's the difference between casual dating and serious dating? Serious dating is dating someone for whom you have very special feelings—someone who, in your opinion, has the qualifications to be a life partner. That's why serious dating should be fun and exciting, but that's also why it's serious business. So serious that I think serious dating should be postponed until at least the last years of high school—for three reasons.

First, there are very few people in their early teens who are emotionally ready to handle the pressures that come with this kind of relationship. Because there are so few who are ready at that age, the likelihood of two of them finding each other is slight—even if you're ready, it isn't likely that your partner will be. Why saddle yourselves with an almost impossible situation when you could be having fun with lots of people?

Second, if you should happen to choose someone to love in your early teens, it will be years before the two of you could marry. Can you be together with someone you love for years without giving in sexually? Only when marriage is a real possibility in the reasonable future should serious relationships be considered. Too many kids are falling into the trap of sexual intimacy before marriage because they start their intimate relationships too early. It's one thing to be able to maintain some sexual self-control when you know that in just a few months you'll be able to give yourself freely to the one you love. It's another thing altogether to control yourselves when you're looking at years before marriage.

The third reason I recommend waiting is that so many serious relationships that start too early are characterized by jealousy, possessiveness, and insecurity. You know that's true if you've ever taken a good honest look around you at the serious relationships your friends may have gotten into. Trust me—you'll be happier if you save serious dating until you can begin to think seriously about marriage in the not-too-distant future.

Don't believe the lie that, if you don't have a steady date, you don't belong in teenage society or that something's wrong with you. Instead, you'll be the winner if you have the courage to wait. You'll be able to look back with fondness at a teenage life of unencumbered fun. The alternative is far less attractive; I rarely run across a young teenage couple who don't in some way feel trapped by their relationship. They tend to hang on to that partner for security long after the relationship has become unhealthy and unsatisfying. This is a terrible misuse of another human being. Don't become trapped.

Because serious business, due to its very nature, involves exploring the possibility of sharing your love with another person, sexual activity will be a temptation. I'll discuss how to handle that temptation in the chapter, "Sex Is Not a Four-Letter Word." The decisions you make about sexual activity — as well as many other decisions you make about serious dating — will affect the rest of your life. Let's talk about some of the important skills you'll need during this important phase of looking for love.

1. *Hold your heart in check.* If casual dating is the time to have carefree fun by test-driving several cars, then serious dating is looking for the right car to buy. Car dealers know that if a person comes on the lot and falls head over heels in love with just one car, they can get that person to pay much more than the car is actually worth. They can also get the customer to overlook obvious flaws, all because that person is overcome with the desire to have *this* car.

Unchecked feelings can cloud your judgment. Unless you can exercise some control over your heart, you'll have a harder time remaining sexually pure, allowing God to control your life, and making sound judgments about the character of the person you are dating. You'll be like the unwise customer on the car lot who can't see that the car he wants so badly just isn't a particularly good one for him. If he'd just let himself test-drive a few other cars, he'd find one that would make him so much happier.

If you let your emotions go before you really get to know the person you're dating, you may pay a very high price. You may miss out on things God is trying to say to you, and you may miss seeing flaws in your partner that will turn out to be disastrous in marriage.

2. *Look for good character.* Does the person you are dating have the characteristics that lead to positive relationships and good marriages?

Is your partner: Kind and loyal? Considerate of others? Disciplined; able to say no in the face of temptation? Even tempered?

Does he or she: Consistently put Christ first? Take the responsibility for knowing where to draw the line with sex, or does he or she keep going until you draw the line?

These qualities, all of which God considers important, are thousands of times more important than good looks. Police files are filled with the horror stories of women who for years were beaten by good-looking husbands. Many of those women saw the danger signs before they were married, but they let their hearts rule. *We love each other,* they thought. *I can change him. He'll listen to me.*

Many men and women are living lonely lives today, separated by divorce from partners who were not loyal. Early in their relationship, they may have recognized those flirtatious tendencies—but chose to ignore them. *We love each other,* they thought. *Our marriage will be so good nothing could threaten it.*

Don't let it happen to you. Watch for the danger signs in the people you date seriously. Possessiveness is one of the most dangerous. If your partner is possessive before marriage, the problem will multiply many times over after marriage. Closely related to possessiveness are jealousy and selfishness. Marriage doesn't solve any of these problems—it magnifies them. If the person you're dating isn't willing to allow God to help him or her deal with these areas, it's time to look for love somewhere else.

If your partner is withdrawn and never shares inner personal feelings, it is time to consider how much further this relationship should go. That doesn't mean you can't be friends; it just means that friendship is as far as that relationship should go. That's why I believe it's so important to draw a very discernible line where friendship stops and the intimacy of serious dating begins. Any friend who reveals unchanging characteristics that would be unacceptable to you in marriage shouldn't be allowed beyond that line.

3. *Have fun.* You'll only be a teenager once. Yes, looking for love is serious business, but you ought to be able to have fun doing it. If dating isn't fun, then something is wrong. One of the reasons I've said the things I've said in this chapter is to help you *enjoy* this stage of your life. My prayer for you right now is that, when you look back on your life, you'll be able to remember this part as one of your most enjoyable times.

Engagement and Marriage

The teenage years are not the years to be saddled with the responsibility of engagement or marriage. Most married teenagers regret making the choice to marry so young.

Does that mean marriage is a horrible, frightening

thing? Of course not. In fact, it's the potential beauty of this union that makes everything I've written above so important. If dating were just a sport, this chapter wouldn't be necessary. But it isn't a sport—it's serious preparation for marriage, and believe me, what happens during your dating life will affect your marriage.

God intended marriage to be the closest and most fulfilling relationship possible between two human beings. In fact, in the Bible, he uses the marriage relationship to describe the relationship he wants to have with the people he loves.

Approach marriage as a lifetime commitment. Use your dating experience to prepare for that commitment. Do that, and your chances of success will be greatly increased.

Tonight as I lie quietly in bed thinking about the things I'm writing to you, the woman that I love is sleeping beside me. She and I have enjoyed life together for over twenty years. What am I feeling for her as I lie here? No great romantic feelings at this particular moment, just a very strong and yet very tender love that has grown between us from facing so many years of life together. There may be other women who are more beautiful, or witty, or talented—but not for me. For me, she's the best, because she is the woman I love. She knows both the good and the bad aspects of my life, and she has chosen to love me anyway. As I listen to her quiet breathing, I pray that God will give us many more years together.

Just before I go to sleep, I will say one more prayer. This one is for you. I pray that you will conduct your quest for love with wisdom and faith, trusting completely in a God who wants only the best for you. More than anything, I pray that you too will experience the kind of love I feel tonight.

God bless you as you look for love.

CHAPTER

6

HANDLING
PEER
PRESSURE

Every day, thousands of teenagers risk their future, the safety of others, and even their own lives by giving in to the powerful pull of peer pressure. Thousands more ignore God's call and find themselves paralyzed, unable to live or share their faith because they are ruled by those around them. Peer pressure has become stronger in their lives than God. Or common sense.

This chapter takes a look at what peer pressure can cost you, and at how to escape its powerful grip.

The Cost of Giving In

I met Debbie after a high-school assembly I'd spoken at. Scar tissue covered the face of this once-beautiful girl. Why? Because one Friday night Debbie did something she didn't want to do, something that she thought was incredibly stupid. She gave in to peer pressure. She's still paying the price for that decision.

A group of her friends decided to have a drinking party after the football game. Although Debbie wasn't a party animal, she didn't want her friends to think she was a prude, so she went along. On a deserted country road they got drunk on black-cherry wine and brandy. Soon all inhibitions were gone, and someone suggested that they play chicken.

You've heard of this crazy game. It's played by driving two cars toward each other at high speed. The first driver to pull out of the path of the other car is chicken and loses the game. That evening, no one pulled away. In the terrible head-on collision, all of Debbie's friends were killed and she was disfigured and crippled for life.

Tears streamed down her face as she told me how much she had wanted to avoid that party. Several times during the

ening, she wanted to ask someone to take her home, but she
as afraid of what her friends would think. Even after the
ame of chicken started, as terrified as she was, she couldn't
mmon the courage to simply ask to get out of the car.

Think of how powerful this thing called peer pressure
The cars had barely missed each other twice before finally
ashing. Debbie realized that her life was in danger; she had
veral chances to get out. Yet she chose to risk her life rather
an risk losing her friends. The sad truth is, I don't think most
the kids in those cars wanted to be there. But they too were
raid to stand out in the crowd. In their unwillingness to speak
it, they signed their own death warrant. These were not bad
ds—these were good kids who gave in to peer pressure and
ade bad decisions.

Behind our church, a set of railroad tracks stretched for
iles. During the lunch break at vacation Bible school one
ar when I was a kid, one of my friends suggested that we put
cks on the tracks and hide in the bushes to see what would
ppen. Nobody had to tell me that was wrong. *What if the
cks derail the train?* I wondered. But like Debbie, I didn't
re speak up.

The first time a train hit those rocks, there was a loud
p and sparks flew in every direction; shrapnel flew through
e woods as we whooped and danced with excitement. Deep
wn I still felt bad about what we were doing, but at the next
eak I was once again out by the track with my friends.

This time, the rocks were bigger and we hid closer to
e tracks. We heard the inspection car coming far enough
vay that we could have removed the rocks. An inspection car,
naller than an automobile, speeds along the tracks looking
r problems that need repair. Each one of us crouched in
ose bushes knew that the rocks we had put on the tracks

could easily derail an inspection car, injuring or even killi
someone—but nobody moved.

When the car hit the rocks, it rolled up on two whe
and almost threw the driver onto the tracks; then it crash
back down safely and screeched to a stop. We ran in eve
direction. Although we were never caught, the scene of th
near disaster ran through my mind many times. What
someone had been hurt or killed? Why didn't I do somethir
I knew that what we were doing was wrong, but I went alo
with it anyway. Peer pressure drove me on.

While working with Youth for Christ in Denv
Colorado, I met a young man who had spent two years ir
juvenile detention center because he had robbed a convenier
store. Dennis was from a good family; he had never been
trouble before.

"Why did you do a thing like that?" I asked him.

"I did it on a dare," he answered. "I didn't want r
friends to think I was chicken."

In Atlanta, a fourteen-year-old girl gave birth to a ba
she didn't want, and two lives were off to a shaky start. Wh
Her boyfriend talked her into having sex; she didn't want
but she didn't have the courage to say no.

In New York, four boys brutally raped and beat
defenseless woman. One of those boys, from a Christi
home, said, "There wasn't anything else to do. I just we
along."

A Christian girl sat in uncomfortable silence as h
friends discussed religion. She didn't share her faith—she w
afraid of what her friends would think.

In Milwaukee, a young man sat in anguish as
considered the claims of Christ. He desperately wanted t
forgiveness and hope that trusting the Lord offers, but
couldn't step out and make that commitment. Why? Becau

I Don't Remember Dropping the Skunk, But . . .

Handling Peer Pressure

he was even more desperate to avoid the criticism and ridicule of his friends.

The cost of giving in to peer pressure is measured in many different ways: prison terms, wasted lives, missed opportunity, tragedy of many kinds, and spiritual bankruptcy. Deep down, every teenager (and every adult) who lives like this knows that their life is without direction. They have allowed the world to push them into its mold. I call that moldy living.

Sound like you sometimes? How do you change that? How do you begin to live your own life?

Choose Who You Will Live For

The first step is to decide, consciously, who you will live for. You could choose to always give in to the pressures around you, but I know of very few people who really want that kind of aimless life. You could also choose to live just for yourself—but there's a problem there: you're likely to end up right back where you started. The goal of serving yourself is often accomplished by giving in to peer pressure. You end up in a vicious cycle.

The best choice is to decide to serve the living God. Not only does this choice give you a clear direction and purpose for your life, but it also taps you into the only power source available to help you live that life. I'm convinced that only through Christ can you emerge victorious as you face the kind of peer pressure you come up against daily. Hebrews 11 tells us about people who faced the worst kind of peer pressure there is, and yet were able to stand strong because of their faith:

> Others were tortured and refused to be released, so that they might gain a better resurrection. Some faced jeers and flogging, while still others were chained and put in prison. They were stoned; they were sawed in two; they were put to death by the

sword. They went about in sheepskins and goatskins, destitute, persecuted and mistreated—the world was not worthy of them. They wandered in deserts and mountains, and in caves and holes in the ground. These were all commended for their faith

Hebrews 11:35–39

Their choice was to live for God.

hoose Principles to Live By

There are lots of people who face each day without a set f principles to guide their decisions and attitudes. Without solid foundation of principles to live by, you'll live by the andards other people force upon you.

People without principles are easy to spot. They live ne kind of life at school, another kind of life at home, and yet nother when they're in church. Because they've let the world ress them into its mold, they change their behavior every time ne mold changes.

Why not let God help you establish your own mold? As ou study the Bible, write down principles that you believe he ants you to live by. And here's a good place to start: When od gave the Ten Commandments to the Israelites, he was roviding a set of principles by which they could guide their ves. Of course, it's God's grace that brings salvation, not the oodness of our lives. Still, those principles God gave the sraelites—the Ten Commandments—will focus your life in ne right direction.

For example: If you live by the principle that you will ot steal, then when the opportunity arises to steal something, won't matter how much you can gain or what pressure your iends are putting on you—your mind will already have been ade up.

My daughter has set the following principle for living: he will never get in the car with someone who has been

Handling Peer Pressure

drinking. Period. It doesn't matter whether it's the parent one of her friends or someone her own age. It doesn't matt if she has to walk or take a taxi. She has set her standard, ar she knows I will back her up. I would rather pay a hundre dollar taxi bill than to have her riding with someone who driving ability is impaired by alcohol.

Setting principles for living will change your prayer li Instead of always asking God to forgive you for giving in peer pressure, you'll be asking for strength to live by what yo know is right. I remember a boy who told me he was prayir that his girlfriend wouldn't get pregnant; meanwhile, continued to have sex with her. Listening to him, I w reminded of one of those passages of Scripture we don't alwa like to hear:

> Do not be deceived: God cannot be mocked. A man
> reaps what he sows. *Galatians 6:7*

That boy was sowing wild oats and praying for cr failure. If he had committed himself to living by the princip that he would not have sex before marriage, then there wou be no reason to mock God with his prayer.

If an area of your life is controlled by peer pressu rather than guided by godly principles, search God's Word f guidance and yield that part of your life to him. It is or through his power that victory is available. You may tempted to pull yourself up by your bootstraps and fix up yo life on your own. All you'll get is broken bootstraps. Make principles—not merely the Ten Commandments, but also t other principles you find in your study of the Bible—t principles by which you live. Write them down so you c review them often.

Giving in to peer pressure doesn't always result

something as terrible as death, disfigurement, or a ruined life. But it does diminish your sense of self-worth. A new boy who was smaller and weaker than me joined our class when I was a sophomore in high school. Since I was the one who was usually beat up at school, I lived in a survival mode. I had few guiding principles in my life and gave in to peer pressure all the time.

One day the new boy accidentally tripped me during a basketball game. I knew he hadn't meant to, but immediately I was surrounded by the boys in my class chanting their encouragement to pay him back. Even though I was a classic "kick-sand-in-his-face" weakling, I had no problem beating this boy silly. At first he fought furiously, but then he began to cry. The gym teacher separated us from the rest of the boys and told us to wait in his office.

I'll never forget the words of that sobbing boy as we sat in the room alone. He wiped the blood from his nose and asked, "Why did you do that? I thought you were a Christian." Like everyone else, he knew some of the principles Christians were supposed to live by. He knew we were supposed to be loving and forgiving. I knew it too, but unfortunately it had never become a principle in my life. That day I *made* it a principle, and even today when I run into a crabby waitress or a rude airline employee I'm reminded of that boy's words and of the principle I have set for my life. That helps me not to blast back. Even when I do fail (That's a secret; don't tell. I don't want anybody else to know I fail occasionally.), the principle helps me get back on track.

Take out a piece of paper before you read another chapter and write down some of the principles you think God wants you to live by. Start with the Ten Commandments, written in your own words, and then use these major headings to help you think of more principles:

Principles for keeping in touch with God
Principles for living with my family
Principles for living for Christ at school
Principles for keeping my body pure for his work
Principles for dating and being with my friends
Principles for how I treat people
Principles for preparing for my future
Principles governing my academic studies
Principles guiding what I will allow into my mind

Keep that piece of paper, and add to it as you read and study his Word. There's no way you can think of every difficult or tempting situation you might someday get into and plan ways to handle it. That's why it's wise to develop broad guidelines that will apply to most situations.

Remember: If you don't set principles for your own life, other people will set them for you. I don't know about you, but I would much rather run my own life with God's help than to wake up at fifty or sixty and realize I let other people run it for me.

Expect Adversity

The third important step is to expect adversity.

Many of us go through life trying to accomplish the impossible: We try to please everyone. Even if you give in to peer pressure, you aren't going to please everyone. That's why the pressure you put on yourself to make everyone happy is one of the greatest pressures you face—and one of the most frustrating, because you'll never succeed. Never. It just can't be done. Whether you choose to live for God, for yourself, or for your friends, you'll never please everyone.

So what are your options? You can try to please everyone by giving in to peer pressure at every turn, and fail

Or you can acknowledge that the way you live isn't going to please everyone, determine that you want a direction for your life, set principles that will guide you in that direction, and face the adversity when it comes.

All of the things we have talked about in this chapter are wonderfully illustrated by the life of Jesus Christ. He came to this earth totally committed to do the will of his Father. He faced peer pressure from the time he could walk. When he was young, his parents questioned his staying behind to teach in the temple. Later in his life, the religious leaders pressured him to change his message, even threatening him with death. (That's what I call real *peer pressure*!) In the wilderness, Satan himself pressured Jesus to use his power to meet his own needs. Finally, as he was dying on the cross, his peers mocked him and pressured him to come down from the cross if he was really the Christ.

But Jesus had come to do his Father's will, and that principle could not be shaken. He had a purpose in life against which every temptation and pressure was weighed. He was prepared to die to accomplish that purpose. Of all the people who have walked the earth, Jesus was the one who least deserved to die. Yet it was the very people that he loved and came to save (his peers) who put him to death. He never hated, he never sought revenge, he never sinned—yet people hated him. Even today, after he has proven his love by his death, and after he has demonstrated his power by his resurrection, there are those who still hate him.

So don't be discouraged by adversity. The purpose for which God created you is worth the struggle. Keep on trusting him. Keep on living by the principles of love he has written in his Word. Don't give in to peer pressure. Give in to him.

Jesus knew that you would run into opposition as you

Handling Peer Pressure

tried to live the Christian life. The Bible has some very encouraging words for you:

> Let us fix our eyes on Jesus, the author and perfecter of our faith, who for the joy set before him [this was the goal that focused his life] endured the cross, scorning its shame [this was the price he had to pay to reach that goal], and sat down at the right hand of the throne of God. Consider him who endured such opposition from sinful men [look at the adversity he faced and still kept going], so that you will not grow weary and lose heart.
>
> *Hebrews 12:2-3*

Keep the faith, my friend.

CHAPTER

7

KNOW HOW
TO HANDLE
YOUR MONEY

My mom used to say, "Never put money in your mouth, because you don't know where it has been."

I never had the urge to put money in my mouth, but I did have the urge to put a lot of it in my pocket. You don't have to worry so much about where money has been; what you have to worry about is where it might take you.

Few things have the power to destroy useful lives as much as the misuse of money. I've seen kids go to jail, I've seen marriages and lives ruined, I've seen faith in God squelched, all over money. You can take courses in high school and college that will teach you a skill or profession that will enable you to make money; you can learn accounting to keep track of how much you make; and you can learn to invest so that you can earn even more money. But where can you learn healthy *attitudes* toward money? Parents are often more lax about teaching their children how to handle money than they are about teaching them how to handle sex. This chapter will reveal how you can use this God-given resource in a way that will provide for your needs and honor him at the same time.

Don't Bow to the Wicked Green Ruler

During a question-and-answer period, a teenager raised his hand. "Doesn't the Bible say somewhere that money is the root of all evil?" he asked me.

I looked around the room; many teenagers were nodding their heads in agreement. I was surprised to see how many in the room thought it was true. The Bible does say something like that, with the addition of one important word. 1 Timothy 6:10-11 says, "For the *love* of money is a root of all kinds of evil. Some people, eager for money, have wandered from the faith and pierced themselves with many griefs. But you, man of God, flee from all this, and pursue righteousness, godliness, faith, love, endurance and gentleness."

This passage of Scripture makes it clear that the *love* of money is the root of all evil. The love of wealth, in any form, will take your eyes from God and lead to a wasted life. Many teenagers tie their self-worth to how much money they have. Others refuse to associate with those in a lower economic class; others live for only one purpose—to accumulate wealth. When money becomes more valuable than your relationship with God, it becomes a source of evil in your life.

Here's a story that illustrates how far this can go. A rich young man had just crashed his very expensive Mercedes and was thrown clear of the wreckage as it disappeared over a cliff. He lost his arm in the accident, and when the police arrived they found him standing at the top of the hill, weeping.

"My Mercedes! My Mercedes!" he howled.

"You ought to be thankful you're alive," the amazed policeman chided.

"But it had twenty thousand dollars worth of options," the young man whimpered as his car burned at the bottom of the cliff.

"There are things that are more important than that stupid car," the angry policeman continued. "We've got to get you to a hospital. Your arm has been torn off—you could bleed to death."

The young man looked down and saw that his arm was missing. With a look of horror, he screamed, "My Rolex! My Rolex!"

A gross exaggeration? The headlines are full of the stories of people who were willing to risk their lives and their future for money. A recent docu-drama told the story of several very wealthy boys who formed a club to cheat people out of money. Their greed reached the point that they resorted to murder to avoid losing what they had gained. No, money is not evil—but the love of money is incredibly evil.

Because wealth allows you to get the things you want it's tempting to let money preempt God in your life. That's why it's important for the Christian to understand that everything he or she has belongs to God. Our wealth is not ours to do with as we please—it's a gift entrusted to us by God to be given back to him when he sees fit.

God wants to be first in your life, and as the Bible says in Exodus 20:5, he's a very jealous God. He doesn't want your clothes or your car or anything else to stand between you and him.

In desperation, a man called out to Christ one night. He wanted to know what he had to do to be saved.

> Now a man came up to Jesus and asked, "Teacher, what good thing must I do to get eternal life?"
>
> "Why do you ask about what is good?" Jesus replied. "There is only One who is good. If you want to enter life, obey the commandments."
>
> "Which ones?" the man inquired.
>
> Jesus replied, "'Do not murder, do not commit adultery, do not steal, do not give false testimony, honor your father and mother,' and 'love your neighbor as yourself.'"
>
> "All these I have kept," the young man said. "What do I still lack?"
>
> Jesus answered, "If you want to be perfect, go, sell your possessions and give to the poor, and you will have treasure in heaven. Then come, follow me."
>
> When the young man heard this, he went away sad, because he had great wealth.
>
> Then Jesus said to his disciples, "I tell you the truth, it is hard for a rich man to enter the kingdom of heaven. Again I tell you, it is easier for a camel to go through the eye of a needle than for a rich man to enter the kingdom of God."
>
> When the disciples heard this, they were greatly astonished and asked, "Who then can be saved?"
>
> Jesus looked at them and said, "With man this is impossible, but with God all things are possible."
>
> *Matthew 19:16–26*

I Don't Remember Dropping the Skunk, But . . .

The man was so attached to his money that he was willing to risk his salvation in order to keep his riches. His riches were worth more to him than life itself. Yet those same riches could guarantee him nothing. Jesus recognized the powerful temptation of riches when he told his disciples that it's easier to get a camel through the eye of a needle than it is to get a rich man into heaven.

Jesus told the following parable of another man who placed his faith in riches, only to discover he had made the wrong choice.

> Then he said to them, "Watch out! Be on your guard against all kinds of greed; a man's life does not consist in the abundance of his possessions."
>
> And he told them this parable: "The ground of a certain rich man produced a good crop. He thought to himself, 'What shall I do? I have no place to store my crops.'
>
> "Then he said, 'This is what I'll do. I will tear down my barns and build bigger ones, and there I will store all my grain and my goods. And I'll say to myself, "You have plenty of good things laid up for many years. Take life easy; eat, drink and be merry."'
>
> "But God said to him, 'You fool! This very night your life will be demanded from you. Then who will get what you have prepared for yourself?'
>
> "This is how it will be with anyone who stores up things for himself but is not rich toward God."
>
> *Luke 12:15–21*

It is dangerous to allow anything to be more important to you than God. Of all the tricks Satan can use to make you less effective for the Lord, this is one of his best. He will encourage you to judge your own worth by what you can accumulate; he will encourage your friends to judge you the same way.

You might be saying, "I don't have a big bank account so this problem doesn't apply to me." Please don't be offended if I ask you some questions that I must continually ask myself:

What are you doing with the money God has given you now?

Do you tithe? (In other words, do you give back to God at least ten percent of your money?)

Do you ever give freely to those who are in need?

Do you spend everything you make on what you want?

If God doesn't have your money, he doesn't really have your life.

Learn to Manage Your Money

The Bible calls managing your money good stewardship. The effort that you put into learning how to manage your money will serve you all your life. Sound useful? Maybe these hints will help you:

1. *Don't get caught in the credit trap.* A popular television commercial shows a happy college student receiving a credit card from her father. Now she'll be able to buy all the things she wants, even when she doesn't have any money. All she needs to do is lay this little piece of plastic on the counter. Some banks are even making it possible for *children* to get credit cards. Be careful—it's a trap. Using credit unwisely for things you don't need can lead to habits of spending that can enslave you for the rest of your life. The key is: *Don't spend money you don't have.*

2. *Fight impulse spending.* Studies have shown that when your mom goes to the supermarket, she'll spend much

...ess if she sticks to a list of the things she needs. Otherwise, when she walks past the attractive displays in the aisles of the store, she'll buy things on impulse that she doesn't need or want.

How many times have you bought something you thought you wanted only to discover that you never use it? Next time you're tempted to buy on impulse, write the item down on a piece of paper and wait thirty days. If you still want it after thirty days, buy it. You'll be amazed how many of those "essentials" you decide not to buy. A few days after you write the name of that item on a piece of paper, you'll realize that you don't really want it so badly after all. By that time you'll have discovered something *else* you think you want—only to discover, after time, that the new thing isn't so important either. Learning to avoid impulse buying will save you much grief later in life. It is good stewardship of God's resources.

3. *Practice tithing.* Now is the time to start giving back to God what is his. Begin setting aside ten percent of your earnings for the Lord now, while you aren't making that much, and you'll find it easier to do later, when your salary increases and those tithe checks start to look much larger. It's easy to rationalize that your little gift isn't very important— hardly worth bothering with. But in Mark 12:41-44, the Lord indicated that he was most pleased with the small gift of a widow.

> Jesus sat down opposite the place where the offerings were put and watched the crowd putting their money into the temple treasury. Many rich people threw in large amounts. But a poor widow came and put in two very small copper coins, worth only a fraction of a penny.
>
> Calling his disciples to him, Jesus said, "I tell you the truth, this poor widow has put more into the treasury than all the others. They all gave out of their wealth; but she, out of her poverty, put in everything—all she had to live on."

Know How to Handle Your Money

4. *Learn to save wisely*. Decide on a percentage of your income to save for a rainy day. And I don't mean that as soon as it rains you should withdraw your savings and spend it. I *do* mean that you can avoid having to buy on credit by preparing for your *needs* ahead of time. For instance, you can begin saving for college now—even if your parents are planning to help you. Remember that when it comes to expenses, you can always expect the unexpected.

Many high-school students have such little understanding of the principle of saving (and such little self-discipline) that they can work the entire summer only to discover they don't have money for school clothes and supplies. They couldn't even save their money a month or two for an expense they knew they would have; they spent their money as fast as they earned it.

The object of saving is not to horde money. There is a difference between saving for a future need and hording. Not long ago a man was found dead of malnutrition in a rat-infested apartment. Hidden in his tiny room was a small fortune. He had horded money all his life, not even using it to meet his basic needs. Some men and women waste their entire life trying to keep wealth they have horded. Some spend their life trying to accumulate as much wealth as possible. And some, through poor management, become slaves just trying to get out of debt. Learning to save wisely will help you to have the money you need when you need it.

5. *Learn to budget*. Budgeting is knowing what your needs are going to be, and planning in advance how you are going to meet those needs.

Few people have any idea of how they actually spend their money. When we had our first child, Diane and I were living on a very small salary. It was only the fact that both of

Know How to Handle Your Money

us were working that made it possible to meet our basic need —or so I thought. Since we would lose over half of our incom when Diane quit her job to have the baby, we expected to hav to sell our home.

Fortunately, we called a Christian friend for som advice. He asked us to keep track of all the money we spent fc a month. We were shocked to discover how much money w were spending on things we didn't need. We were wastin hundreds of dollars on pop alone! It was no big deal, folks, t cut back on pop so that we could afford things like electricity water, a phone, and a house.

We learned from that experience that one income wa enough to live on if we followed a careful budget. (We notice something else during that experience, too—we had stoppe giving to the Lord. It was exciting to begin to give to him agai out of the plenty he had supplied to us.) We still live in tha house today. I was very grateful to that friend who took th time to show us how to be good stewards of God's resources By making some minor adjustments and by planning what w could spend, we actually started living better than before—o less money.

Do you like challenges? Here's one: Keep track of ever penny you make and how you spend it over a period of abou three months. Don't trick yourself into thinking that you onl have to keep track of the big things; you'll quickly discover tha a lot of money slips through your fingers in tiny amounts.

Plan ahead for the things you need; determine hov much you'll have to save in order to buy those things. Mak sure you plan your tithe into the budget.

6. *Learn the beauty of giving.* I was deeply moved b a news story of a very poor boy who had spent his entire saving to help someone in need. He had been saving his pennies fc months to buy a Boy-Scout uniform, but one night on the television news he learned about a boy his age whose bicycle had been stolen. The boy who'd been saving for the Boy-Scout uniform sent all his money to help the other boy buy a new bicycle.

In the days that followed, hundreds of people who were moved by his generosity sent donations so that the generous little boy could get his Boy-Scout uniform. When he first donated his savings, of course, that boy didn't expect to be repaid—he only knew that someone was in need, and he was willing to sacrifice to help him.

A beautiful story, isn't it? It was followed on the news by the story of a millionaire who was evicting hundreds of poor people from their homes so that he could make even more millions on a real-estate deal. No one was moved by the greedy behavior of the New York millionaire; no one listening to the news that night sent him money to help him put together his deal. The richest people in the world are people who care about and respond to the needs of other people around them.

There are few things in life that bring the pleasure that this kind of giving brings. Allow the Holy Spirit to show you those who are in need. When he does, be ready to give, even if it means that you might have to do without something that you want.

7. *Give to others freely.* While visiting third-world countries, Bart Campolo and his father, Tony, have often been invited as guests into the homes of people living there. Even though these people had no money and food was scarce, they have usually offered Bart and his father a meal. Although, by U.S. standards, we might consider the meal meager, Bart realized that his hosts would probably go hungry for many days—they were sharing everything they had. This is the kind

Know How to Handle Your Money

of giving that God loves.

God doesn't promise that if you give your money and resources, he will give money and resources back to you. That's a popular concept today, but it isn't true. What you *will* get from giving is more valuable than all the riches of the world put together. You'll get the blessing that only comes from sharing with another child of God what God was gracious enough to give to you in the first place.

I have never met a teenager who has given sacrificially that hasn't been changed for the better because of it. Whether they gave time and sweat to a work project or shared their belongings with others, without exception they speak of the experience with a special look in their eye. They learned from that experience what many people never learn in their entire lifetime: that life is more than just getting whatever you can. Instead, life gives us a chance to share the love of Christ with others by giving. What else *can* we do, after all he has done for us?

All my life, I'll remember sitting at a hamburger place with three friends in high school. Only one boy had a job and money. He ordered three hamburgers for himself and proceeded to eat all three in front of us. Our growling stomachs must have sounded like an approaching thunderstorm, yet as he wolfed those hamburgers down, it never occurred to him what he was doing. We weren't starving (although it would have been hard to convince us of that at the moment), but we were hungry enough that it was agony watching him eat. He was blind—totally unaware that sharing those hamburgers with his friends would have been a lot more fun than eating them by himself. Our friendship was never the same after that.

In contrast, consider a boy named Trevor. Trevor

njoyed all the things boys his age enjoy, but one day he saw
mething that would change his life forever. His heart was
ripped by the image of the homeless men and women he saw
ing in the streets. Trevor wasn't rich, and he wasn't old
nough to start a fancy program to help those people, but he
ouldn't get the sight of those shivering people out of his
ind.

One night he gave one of those homeless men the only
ing he had to give—a blanket. The joy Trevor gained from
ving that simple gift, coupled with the visible need of other
eople spending cold nights on the street, led him to ask his
arents if they would help. Trevor could have forced that
oncern out of his mind, but instead he responded to the tug
at God placed in his heart. Responding in that way cost
revor something; it cost him more than a blanket. He ended
p sacrificing time that could have been spent playing baseball,
e gave up some of his privacy, and at times he even risked
ersonal harm. Why? Because he saw people in need, and he
as willing to give some of what he had to help those people.

At the time, he had no idea that his efforts would bring
m national attention. All he knew was that people were in
eed, and he was willing to help. As a result of his obedience
God, thousands of people have responded to that same tug
their own hearts and helped build a place that meets the
eeds of hundreds of hungry, homeless people. It's called
revor's Place.

Trevor will be the first to tell you that everything is not
oses. He pays a high price for his generosity. He will also tell
ou that what keeps him going is not the attention he receives,
ut the joy that Christ gives when you reach out beyond
ourself.

But if you wait until you think you have enough to give,

Know How to Handle Your Money

it will never happen.

The same kind of thing happened when Jesus wa[s] preaching to a huge crowd and there wasn't enough food t[o] feed them all. A small boy had brought with him a small lunc[h] of bread and fish. When Jesus asked for help, the boy wa[s] willing to share what little he had. He could have reasoned th[at] the people should have had enough foresight to bring the[ir] own lunch. He could have rationalized that his little lunc[h] wouldn't make a dent in the appetites of several thousan[d] people, and just kept it for himself. Instead, he shared what h[e] had. God then did what he loves to do: He turned that sma[ll] lunch into enough food to feed five thousand people.

And he has done the same thing with Trevor's blanke[t.] He has turned it into a place of love and hope for hundreds [of] homeless men and women—Trevor's House.

What do you have to share? Be assured that, whateve[r] it is, it is enough for God to multiply.

CHAPTER

8

SEX IS NOT
A FOUR-
LETTER WORD

What *is* this thing called sex that affects you from the time you are born until the day you draw your last breath?

That's a good question—and, because people find out about sex from many different sources, they come up with many different answers to that question. Some kids learn about sex from what they find written on bathroom walls. Others learn by listening to their classmates. Junior-high boys are experts on the subject, and teach each other everything they know.

I learned about sex from my cousin. We were walking down a road throwing stones at the birds lined up on the telephone wires, when we came to a field full of cattle. Close to the road, a bull was breeding a cow. We rolled on the ground and laughed until I thought my sides would split.

What was so funny? I admit that a bull breeding a cow is not a particularly pretty sight, but neither is it a high moment in comedy. As I look back, I think I was laughing because I felt confused and stupid. I grew up on a farm, so I had seen this before—without laughing. I had even helped with the delivery of several calves, which deep down inside had stirred a curiosity about my own sexual makeup. But believe it or not, until that day with my cousin, I had never put two and two together. It was easier to laugh than to risk being laughed at by revealing my ignorance.

After the bull had completed his performance and we had exhausted all the crude comments we could think of, my cousin turned to me and said, "That's what your father did to your mother to get you."

I hit him in the face. As he fell to the ground, I was right on top of him, pummeling with both fists. "Don't you ever say that about my mom and dad!" I screamed.

He started to laugh at me. The more he insisted it was

ue, the madder I got. All my life I had thought of sex as something crude and dirty. My parents weren't crude and dirty, nor were they cows, so how could he say they would do such a thing?

Before long, of course, I discovered that my cousin was right. But those first impressions of sex—that it was something to be sneered and laughed at—stayed with me for a long, long time.

If you look around, you'll quickly find other confusing views of sex. In TV commercials, sex is simply a gimmick for selling everything from cars to beer. Television and movies present sex as a fun thing to do with friends—or even strangers. And then there's pornography, a twisted lie that, unfortunately, some teenagers fall prey to, never learning the real truth. Depending on how you were raised, you may believe that sex is either a beautiful expression of love between married people or an evil necessity you must endure to keep the earth populated. Sigmund Freud, a man who had a profound influence on psychiatry, believed sex was at the center of all the decisions we make. But who made sex, and what is it really?

Brief History of Sex

For much of my youth, I was certain that someone besides God had created sex. I thought that God gave us all the normal stuff, and then when he took a coffee break, Satan snuck in and gave us the sex organs and all the feelings that make them work. What else *can* you think when you believe that sex is dirty? And, I must admit, there were times when that feeling was reinforced by the teaching of well-meaning Christians who, out of their frustration at seeing lives destroyed by the misuse of sex, tried to protect me by teaching me that it was dirty so I would avoid it altogether. But that, too, is a

Sex is Not a Four-Letter Word

misuse of sex, and it, too, can destroy lives.

The truth is: God made sex, and he made it to b[e] enjoyed by the creatures he loved so much. It is one of th[e] greatest expressions of love two people can share. But man h[as] twisted God's creation. Instead of acknowledging that Go[d] made sex and following his guidelines for its use, we have mad[e] sex our god and allow our lives to revolve around it.

Some cultures put likenesses of their gods everywher[e.] So do we—we put sex everywhere. It's on almost all advertisin[g] billboards, on nearly every television show, rarely missing fro[m] the movies and plays you watch, and it's the major subject [of] conversation at most schools. In the midst of all that, is [it] possible to find a balanced view of sex that doesn't deny o[ur] own sexuality and yet doesn't emphasize sex at the expense [of] everything else? Yes, it is. Let's take a look at the truth abo[ut] sex. Then we'll examine some steps you can take to understan[d] and live with your own sexuality.

Don't Underestimate Sex

The definition of sex is often limited to the act of sexu[al] intercourse. Nothing could be further from the truth. Th[e] beauty of your sexuality started long before you were eve[n] aware of the opposite sex, and it continues far beyond the a[ct] of intercourse.

When you were a child and first experienced the warm[,] reassuring touch of your mother and the secure, firm hug [of] your father, those feelings were a part of your sexual makeu[p.] They were the first building blocks that would later enable yo[u] to love and to be loved. Those feelings had nothing to do wi[th] being turned on—but they were sexual feelings nevertheles[s.] When you terrified your mother and father the first time yo[u] discovered your own sexual organs, those also were sexu[al] feelings—even though you didn't know what the things you had discovered were for. You shocked your parents because they identified all sexual feelings with eroticism; they couldn't see that you were simply and innocently curious.

Even within marriage, sex extends far beyond the act of intercourse. I'm as alive and normal as the next guy on the block, but if I had to choose between never having sexual intercourse again and never having the warm, accepting love that is communicated and demonstrated in hugs, glances, and the quiet moments of just holding each other, I would give up intercourse in a moment.

I can just hear you saying, "No you wouldn't."

Oh, yes I would.

Now you're saying, "You must be crazy!"

No, I'm not crazy.

Now you're saying, "Yes, but you are old."

Compared to you I may be old, but my sex drive is alive and well. I'm not saying that sexual intercourse isn't enjoyable or important. I am saying that it is not the most important aspect of marriage, nor does it even come close to being enough to hold a marriage together. Sexual intercourse is only one part of sex. The *strongest* aspects of love go far beyond the bedroom.

Tony Campolo has put it beautifully in a letter he wrote to his son. He was trying to describe the incredible love he felt for his wife.

> When I was in graduate school studying the sociology of the family, my professors often made the point that good sexual relationships usually came from good interpersonal relationships. I remember one of my favorite teachers, James H. S. Bossard, regularly poking fun at those in the field of family studies to whom he referred as being in the "pure orgasm school of thought."

Sex is Not a Four-Letter Word

His sarcasm was aimed at those in the field who overemphasize the importance of being well-informed about sex as a prerequisite to successful marriages and healthy psychological adjustment. Bossard argued convincingly that ours is a society in which people have become experts on how to relate physically but are sadly inept at relating to each other as persons. He went on to contend that if a man and a woman develop a deep love and respect for each another, all else will follow. It was his belief that if a man and woman develop a profound friendship (that's right—I said "friendship"), a sexual adjustment is likely to follow. Conversely, Bossard was convinced that sexual problems that occur between husbands and wives are much more likely to be the result of things that have gone wrong with their friendship than because of anything wrong with them physically or any lack of knowledge of the best techniques of foreplay or positioning ...

Tony went on to tell his son:

> I did all that I could to let you know that being married was the most fulfilling experience that a person could have. Mom was my best friend, and I did my best to make you conscious of that reality.
> –from *Things I Wish We Had Said*, by Anthony and Bart Campolo.

Like Tony, I want to make you conscious that you are a sexual being capable of giving love far beyond just the physical act of sex. If intercourse were the ultimate expression of love, then the most happy people on the earth would be prostitutes and people who are sexually promiscuous. Instead those sad people find it almost impossible to love or to be loved.

Within the intimate commitment of marriage, sex becomes a powerful expression of unity. God calls it becoming one flesh. Your own feelings may tell you that true satisfaction

Sex Is Not a Four-Letter Word

will only come if you follow the current trend and hop into the sack with your date. Those feelings lie. "Going all the way" is not fifteen minutes of ecstasy in the back seat of a car. Yesterday, I watched two old people who had been married for forty-one years as they sat quietly talking in the park. They may not even remember what the back seat of a car looks like, but when those two friends and lovers stood and locked arms as they walked away, I thought, "Any love that lasts *that* long is 'going all the way.'"

My wife recently lost twenty pounds. She found that she was eating to relieve boredom and stress. Yet eating did not relieve her boredom; it only made her grow overweight. To remind herself that eating would not give her what she was really looking for, she taped a message to the front of the refrigerator that said, "It isn't in here." Whenever she was tempted, the note reminded her of the truth.

I would be a liar to suggest that there is no pleasure associated with premarital sex. But the real love and passion that you desire in a relationship—I guarantee it—can't be found there. Just to remind yourself of that, maybe it would be a good idea to put a little sign in the car or on a bracelet that says, "It isn't here."

Sex is at its very best when it's used the way God intended. Don't be fooled by lies, and don't let your feelings trick you into living just for the moment. God, the inventor, wrote the guidelines for the best sex. The beauty of sex can be enjoyed most when you understand its total scope rather than concentrating on just one aspect of sexual expression. If your view of sex is too narrow, you will assume that your deepest sexual longings can be satisfied if you just get into bed with someone. Wrong. That will, in fact, lead to great dissatisfaction.

In this book I will sometimes use the word *sex* to mean sexual intercourse. Just remember, then and always, that your sexuality goes far beyond that.

Know What the Bible Says About Sex?

The Bible makes it clear that sex was designed by God for a very good purpose. It speaks with passion—in very positive terms—about this expression of love within marriage. But the Bible is just as clear about sexual immorality.

> Do you not know that the wicked will not inherit the kingdom of God? Do not be deceived: Neither the sexually immoral nor idolaters nor adulterers nor male prostitutes nor homosexual offenders nor thieves nor the greedy nor drunkards nor slanderers nor swindlers will inherit the kingdom of God.... The body is not meant for sexual immorality, but for the Lord, and the Lord for the body.... Flee from sexual immorality. All other sins a man commits are outside his body, but he who sins sexually sins against his own body. Do you not know that your body is a temple of the Holy Spirit, who is in you, whom you have received from God? You are not your own: You were bought at a price. Therefore honor God with your body.
>
> *1 Corinthians 6:9–10, 13, 18–20*

Sex outside of marriage is labeled as sin. But does that make sense? Why would God create a desire so strong only to say it's wrong to act on that desire? Does he want to keep you from enjoying life?

Hardly. God created sex to be used and enjoyed, not to be ignored. But he created it to be used *within* marriage as an expression of total commitment and unity. The ecstasy of

Sex is Not a Four-Letter Word

sexual intercourse is at its peak as an expression of this kind of love. The excitement of sex outside of marriage cannot approach the joy of sex as God meant it to be. When he set the guidelines, he didn't design them to prevent you from enjoying sex, but rather to enable you to experience sex *at its best*.

In that case, is it okay for unmarried people to do everything *except* intercourse? Is anything okay as long as you don't "go all the way?" There are some problems there. The first problem is that it's almost impossible to do—most kids who have tried it find that they eventually give in and have intercourse anyway.

But what if you *can* stop? There are teenagers who, time and time again, lead each other on only to stop just short of intercourse. Unfortunately, many of these people establish a pattern that can't be easily changed when they get married. Now that they're free to enjoy each other sexually, they can't. There is strong and consistent evidence that having sex before marriage distorts and diminishes the power of this expression of love within a marriage. Yet bringing each other to the point of intercourse and then stopping can be very destructive as well.

Set Guidelines That Will Help You

If you choose to obey God's directives concerning sex, it's important to establish a game plan. Lots of teenagers start with good intentions. They want to be pure; they have a desire to save themselves for marriage. But they're not sure how to accomplish that goal, so they decide to play it by ear. "I'll deal with the problem when it happens."

Wrong!! Without a game plan, this is one battle you're going to lose. The sexual drive is a very powerful force.

Waiting to deal with this issue until you're in a difficult situation is like rolling a snowball down a mountain and telling yourself you'll figure out some way to stop it when you get near the bottom. There *are* several places you can stop that snowball—if you've planned ahead. But at some point halfway down the mountain, that snowball will have picked up enough speed, weight, and momentum that it will be almost impossible to stop.

Likewise, you don't wait until your heavy breathing has the windows of the car steamed up to decide that this is the time to stop. Set limits ahead of time, and determine never to go beyond them.

Now you want me to tell what the limits are, right? I can't do that. Instead, I'll give you some suggestions that will help you stay within the guidelines set in the Bible—but ultimately, it is *you* who must decide where the lines will be drawn. This is where your relationship with Christ really starts to make a difference in your life. If he is first in your life and if you are committed to doing his will, you'll be conscious of what he wants and be able to make intelligent decisions.

So How Far Is Too Far?

The term *foreplay* is used to describe the activities that God intended to prepare a man and woman for sexual intercourse. Foreplay gives the snowball a giant push downhill. These activities are all part of foreplay: embracing with body language, prolonged passionate kissing (especially French kissing), and the fondling of breasts and genitals. You may have heard this called making out or petting (not to be confused with petting your cat).

Regardless of what you call it, it's more than just a way to pass time. These activities were designed to lead to intercourse. And let me add one other thing to that list: erotic conversation, which includes talking about sex, or even more dangerous, talking about having sex together. I know of a Christian couple who had set very high standards for their relationship but eventually gave in because of talk. They would sit for hours together talking about the sexual freedom they would enjoy when they were married. That would be enough to make a saint come unglued.

Foreplay—including all of those things listed above —isn't advisable before marriage because the end result is either intercourse or sexual frustration, two things God has asked the Christian to avoid. At whatever stage you feel yourself heading in the direction of intercourse, it's important to stop.

Jay Kesler, who has helped many teenagers deal with this issue, gave some helpful advice when he suggested that you never allow your partner to unzip, unbutton, or unsnap any part of your clothing. Of course, you could find many loopholes to this advice by going between the buttons, beneath the clothing, or just ripping the clothes off. And there will be times when the sex urge is so strong that is exactly what you would like to do.

The point is to set the limits at a place where you can still handle your emotions. If you continually see how far you can go without going "all the way," eventually you'll give in. The time to stop is the moment you begin to feel sexually stimulated. Your limits may vary slightly from night to night. For example, on a particularly romantic night you may find your emotions running away just by being embraced. If so, then that's the time to recognize your vulnerability and tighten your limits while you can still think straight.

Condition Your Mind to Purity

If you vow to remain pure in your relationships but allow your mind to continually dwell on sexual impurity, you'll be defeated before you even begin. If you choose to indulge in outright pornography to satisfy your sexual urges, then you'll lose on two fronts. First, your sexual behavior is bound to be influenced by the sexual behavior you see portrayed in the pornography you view. Don't fool yourself; you think you can expose yourself to it and walk away unchanged, but that isn't the way pornography works. You begin first to think and later to act like the models in the pornographic material. And second, pornography more than anything else has a way of destroying the joy of the real thing. Its twisted view works like a virus to change the beauty of sex into a degrading, unfulfilling lie.

Avoid pornography like the plague it is, and instead focus on the beauty of God-ordained purity, intended to make your future relationship with your spouse all that it can be.

Avoid Sexually Stimulating Situations

Imagine yourself praying with your boyfriend or girlfriend, asking God to help you remain pure, and then popping some really sensual video into the VCR. Not wise. You'll be allowing what you watch to frustrate both of you. If you've reached a point in your relationship that you're struggling with staying pure, make careful choices about what you watch together. It's also a good idea to limit the times when you're alone and to make sure that you're alone only in places where sexual intimacy would be inconvenient.

I know, I know—that sounds really weird, maybe even impossible. Some of you must wonder what planet I come from. You may even wonder if I have any real blood or hormones in my body. I come from the planet Earth and I do

Sex is Not a Four-Letter Word

have blood and hormones. That's why I'm writing this. I've been through the same things you're going through, and I've made some bad decisions. Some of those decisions, and many of the attitudes I brought into my marriage, came close to destroying the true love that holds my marriage together.

The kind of discipline I'm suggesting is not without some pain and frustration of its own. When every fiber in your body is crying out to go ahead, it takes supernatural help to do what's right. But in the long run, it's worth it. If you give it all away now, what's left for the man or woman you choose to love for the rest of your life? The fact that someone turns you on isn't a good enough reason to allow that person to plunder your body.

Seek Out Partners Who Have Similar Standards

If you expect to remain sexually pure, make sure the people you're dating have the same standards as you. I don't think that any Christian should consider serious dating with anyone but another Christian who is also committed to waiting until marriage.

Don't be afraid to make your standards known early in the relationship. That's much easier than waiting until the windows begin to fog up. A commitment that the two of you make together will be more meaningful and easier to maintain. For example, a girl might say to her boyfriend, "I really like you and want to spend time with you. But I've set some standards for my life that are very important to me, and if you like me I hope they'll be important to you as well. When I say no, please believe that I mean it and don't press me beyond that. If you respect my standards, it will make it much easier for me to get to know you better."

Unfortunately, in our society it's considered okay for the man to press as far as he can, leaving the difficult decision of where to stop up to the woman. Guys, here's a challenge for you—set your own standards and take the initiative to verbalize those standards early in the relationship. Something as simple as: "I think that God wants me to wait until marriage before having sex. I want you to know that so you'll understand that, if I don't pursue things when it gets a little heated, it's not because I don't care. It's because I care very much. Please trust me and help me. This is something I hope we can work on together." A partner who's willing to work toward keeping the relationship within the guidelines set by God is one that is worth keeping.

Use Your Head

It's easy to follow wherever your glands are leading. But one of the elements that separates humans from animals is intelligence. Discipline requires that you use that God-given intelligence to make good decisions in the face of temptation.

Ann Landers received this letter:

Dear Ann,
I have been sleeping with three women for several months. Until a few days ago, none of them knew that the others existed and things were going fine. By chance, two of them met each other, compared notes, and found me out. Now they are furious with me. What am I going to do?
P.S. Please don't give me any of your moral junk.
                                    Signed, Trapped.

Ann Landers answered like this:

Dear Trapped,
The one major thing that separates the human race from animals is a God-given sense of morality. Since you don't have a sense of morality, I strongly suggest you consult a veterinarian.

Don't allow your glands to run your life. Use your head.

Don't Be Discouraged

I felt like a total outcast in high school because I was sure that I was the only virgin boy in my class. I thought I was some kind of weirdo. It wasn't until long after I graduated that I discovered the truth. Everybody *isn't* doing it—but everybody is *saying* they are doing it.

Many teenagers are experimenting with sex, it's true—but not all of them. As Josh McDowell points out in his presentations on sexuality, once your virginity is gone, it's gone forever. What a gift to save for the one you'll marry! That's not being prudish; it's being prudent. Don't be discouraged. Your purity will be rewarded. And you are not alone.

If, as you read this chapter, you feel discouraged because you have already been sexually involved, take heart. God offers you his complete forgiveness. And though it won't be easy, he will also give you the strength to live within his guidelines. The passage from 1 Corinthians I quoted earlier finishes like this:

> Neither the sexually immoral nor idolaters nor adulterers nor male prostitutes nor homosexual offenders nor thieves nor the greedy nor drunkards nor slanderers nor swindlers will inherit the kingdom of God. *And that is what some of you were. But you were washed, you were sanctified, you were justified in the name of the Lord Jesus Christ and by the Spirit of our God.* (italics added)
>
> *1 Corinthians 6:9-11*

Even if this chapter has frustrated or angered you, this is an important issue—don't shrug it off. For a more detailed look at the importance of waiting till marriage that may answer more of your questions or give more specific guidelines on how to make that goal a reality, I highly recommend two books: Josh McDowell's *Why Wait?* (Here's Life Publishers, 1987) and *Worth the Wait*, by Tim Stafford (Campus Life/Zondervan, 1989).

CHAPTER

9

HOW TO
DEVELOP
PERSONAL
INTEGRITY

Personal integrity is absolutely essential for championship living. If you tell the truth, keep your promises, and live an open and honest life, you'll be sought out as a friend who, to borrow a phrase from Garrison Keillor, is definitely above average. This chapter will present three steps to developing that kind of integrity in your life.

Learn to Tell the Truth

For years my father and other "skunk experts" told me that if you pick up a skunk by its tail it can't squirt you. Their theory was that it's only while skunks are standing on the ground that they possess some mysterious leverage that enables them to display (or should I say *dispray*) their God-given ability.

It was all a lie. On the way to church one June morning, I discovered the real truth. A family of skunks appeared in front of the car, and my father gave me the honor of catching a small one for a pet. I had several doubts. First, how could a skunk ever make a good pet? If what my father told me was true, you would have to hang him by his tail—and who really wants a skunk hanging there as a conversation piece in the living room? You could pet him while he was hanging there, but if you took him for a walk you'd have to swing him by his tail, because heaven forbid that you ever let those back feet touch the ground.

Second, there is no such thing as a small skunk. A skunk is measured by its ability, not by its size. Even a flea with that ability would be a BIG skunk.

Third, skunks can do anything they want whenever they want.

I know the truth now, but the day the skunks crossed the road I believed all the lies. So when my father said, "Go git 'em," I went to git 'em. With confidence I grabbed the nearest skunk by the tail, lifted that little (?) creature right off the ground, and brought the business end of his gifted body up to eye level. I am convinced that this skunk knew about the lies. Looking back, I'm sure I saw just the hint of a smile as he turned to be sure of his aim.

The last thing I remember was a fine mist of spray. I don't remember dropping the skunk, but I do remember trying to breathe. The government should require that a skunk have a label on its backside that reads, "DO NOT USE NEAR EYES, NOSE, MOUTH, OR CIVILIZATION OF ANY KIND." This stuff was terrible.

Needless to say, my social life dropped off immediately. In church they gave me a "pew" to myself.

Then the lies started again. They said there were three ways to get rid of skunk smell:

1. *Wash in tomato juice.* That's another lie! It cost a fortune, I still smelled terrible, and it made the tomato juice taste awful.

2. *Burn the affected material.* That worked great with my clothes, but I wasn't quite ready to purify my body that way.

 3. *Bury the affected material.* This could be hazardous to one's health. And besides, I have a sneaking suspicion that, when those who were buried to get rid of skunk smell get to heaven, the Lord will meet them at the gate and say, "I'm sorry, you were told a lie—you'll have to burn."

I got sprayed two more times in my life before I learned the *real* truth. The best way to avoid being sprayed by skunks is to *stay away from them altogether.*

We finally bought a German shepherd and let him fight with the skunks. When he got all stunk up, he would lie

How to Develop Personal Integrity

on the porch, and I would pick him up by the hind legs, throw him off the porch—and never get sprayed.

What's the point? The point is that *no matter how you try to handle a lie, you're going to get skunked*. The solution? Avoid the lies.

At the very foundation of personal integrity is a commitment to the truth. Once people know that you lie, they can no longer trust you. You may be saying, "But I don't lie to my friends." The truth is that if your friends know you lie to others, they have no way of knowing you won't lie to them.

On the other hand, if they see that you always tell the truth, even when it hurts, then even when all of the evidence is against you, your word will be enough—they'll know you can be trusted.

Often we get so used to telling "little white lies" that we don't realize we're doing it. For instance, I tend to exaggerate. I want to impress people, and sometimes I'm afraid the truth won't be impressive enough, so I add to it. Instead of saying that I flew 250,000 miles last year, I want to say that I flew 300,000. After all, what's 50,000 miles between friends? And it sounds so much more impressive.

But like any other kind of lie, exaggeration can backfire. I was embarrassed several years ago when I was caught in one of those "little white lies." I had just started running for exercise when I met a young lady who was also a runner. I was running six miles a day, six days a week. That's a total of 36 miles a week. Not bad. But because I wanted to impress this lady with my athletic ability (and, believe me, the only way to impress anyone with my athletic ability is to lie), I told her that I ran one hundred-and-twenty miles a week.

My first clue that she didn't believe me was when she

spit her coffee all over me as she burst out laughing. The conversation, which had been interesting to that point, was over. My little exaggeration was taken for what it really was: a lie. I thought about saying, "Did I say one hundred-and-twenty miles a week? Silly me! What I meant was one hundred and-twenty miles a *year*!" But it was too late. I had already made a fool of myself.

Most exaggerations are so small we don't get caught. We rationalize by saying, "I only lied a little." That's like saying, "I'm a little bit pregnant." There is no such thing as a little pregnant, a little skunk, or a little lie. Think back to the last time you met someone who was exaggerating. Did you admire that person? Did you find yourself wanting to spend more time with him? Think before you speak, and resolve not to exaggerate at all.

Always telling the truth is like putting money in the bank. Call it a *trust* fund. It may require discipline, and sometimes it can be painful, but when you need to make a withdrawal, the *trust* will be there.

God has some very strong views on lying. The ninth commandment in Exodus 20:16 reads: "You shall not give false testimony against your neighbor." This commandment was given because God knew how lies destroy relationships. In Ephesians 4:25 Paul wrote, "Stop lying to each other; tell the truth, for we are parts of each other and when we lie to each other we are hurting ourselves" (The Living Bible). Even if you never get caught in a specific lie, lying will eventually snare you.

So it's up to you. Do you want to be known as a person of integrity—someone who can be trusted? Then make a commitment not to lie.

Learn to Live Honestly

If you live a lie, you will tell a lie.

It's easier to avoid lying if you live the kind of life that doesn't *require* lying. As a high-school student, I found myself living one way at church, another way at school, and still another at home. Many of my friends in school didn't know of my commitment to Christ. I didn't *want* them to know. And when I was with those friends, I would do things I knew were wrong to prove I was one of the gang. On Sunday I would stand up and testify to the power of Christ in my life, but if the people in church had seen the way I behaved in school, they would have seen no evidence of that power. Sometimes, frankly, my expressions of faith were a lie designed to fool my parents into believing I was the good little boy they expected me to be. And my life at school was a lie, too, since I didn't really believe in what I was doing and saying there. I was living a lie.

There are two basic steps to living honestly:

First: *Squarely face who you are and don't pretend to be something else.*

In chapter 1 we talked about discovering the real you. Step one above requires that you *be* the real you. And that's scary. After all, if you let people know who you really are, they might reject that person. On the other hand, putting on a mask seems safe. If people reject that mask, at least you know they weren't rejecting the real you. But how sad to go through life with the real you never being known by anyone.

The risk of being rejected is far less painful than the loneliness of never being known.

Here's a typical conversation:

Debbie: "Hi, I'm Debbie. You're new here, aren't

you?" (I hope this is someone who has the same values I have. But I don't want to tip my hand too soon or he may reject me.)

Bill: "Yeah, I am. I'm Bill. Didn't I see you at the game Wednesday?" (I'd better be careful and stay on neutral ground.)

Debbie: "Yeah, what a game, huh?" (I love to *play* basketball more than watch it, but I suppose he would think I'm an Amazon if I told him. I better keep quiet.)

Bill: "Who was that group of kids you were with? They weren't from our school, were they?" (That looked like the kind of group I would like to be part of.)

Debbie: (Uh, oh—if he finds out that was my church youth group he'll think I'm a religious nut and this won't go any further.) "Just a bunch of friends."

Bill: "Looked like you guys were having a great time." (Sure wish I could find a friend who wanted to follow God like I do. I could really use the support.)

Debbie: (My friends are wonderful, but if I stay on this subject he'll find out about my faith.) "Yeah, they're okay. Are you going to the dance on Saturday?" (I'd much rather just spend a nice evening talking, but I'm sure he'd never go for that.)

Bill: "I wouldn't miss it. I love to party." (I *hate* those parties. I'd much rather spend a quiet evening talking, but I have to make the right impression.)

Debbie: "Maybe I'll see you there." (Who am I trying to kid? I'm not even going, but at least this gets me out of this conversation. Guess I was right about his tastes. How I wish I could find someone who has the same interests I do.)

Bill: "Nice meeting you, Debbie. I'll see you Saturday." (No, I won't. I'm not going to any party. Too bad—she seemed so nice. I wish she liked the things I like. Oh, well. I'll

I Don't Remember Dropping the Skunk, But . . .

just keep looking.)

What could have been the start of a good relationship ends prematurely because these kids insisted on wearing a mask instead of taking the risk to be real. They started and ended their relationship with a lie. What's even sadder is that some relationships go on for years without the masks ever coming off.

I lied on all fronts of my life. I was a very weak Christian, but I didn't want my pastor or my parents to know that, so I put on a mask. When they asked me, "Is everything okay?" I would answer, "Yes." I desperately wanted to be a better Christian, but my "little white lie" took away any opportunity for them to help me. Unless you establish a habit of being honest about yourself, you will carry that lonely addiction to lying right into adulthood.

When I first entered the world of entertainment, I quickly began to live a double standard. I was made acutely aware of the lie I was living when the people from my two different worlds began to mix. When people from church came to see my show, I would change my behavior dramatically so they wouldn't see how I was living.

One Sunday, to my surprise, one of my fellow entertainers came to my church. When he saw me, he was as surprised as I was; his eyes widened and he said, "What are *you* doing here?" Here was a person trying to find some meaning in life. I knew that the answer he was seeking was in Jesus Christ, but I was living a lie that made me powerless to help him. In fact, I was a hindrance.

I went home that day and wept, asking God's forgiveness and praying for his strength to live the truth.

Some of you might be thinking, "All right, then. I'll just live a wild and free life and do whatever I want and not care what anybody thinks. At least I'll be honest. No masks." Wrong. That life-style turns the truth of God into a lie. It's downright dangerous to continue to sin and think, "That's just the way I am." The very power of the Holy Spirit and the meaning of Christ's death on the cross is mocked by that lie.

Honest living is the acknowledgment that we are weak, coupled with the desire to allow God to help us overcome that weakness. Paul talks about the attitude that characterizes honesty in Romans 7:18: "For I have the desire to do what is good, but I cannot carry it out. For what I do is not the good I want to do; no, the evil I do not want to do—this I keep on doing." Paul doesn't just recognize his weak and sinful nature and leave it at that. He refuses to give in to it—and he challenges us to do the same.

In Romans 6:12–14, Paul says: "Therefore do not let sin reign in your mortal body so that you obey its evil desires. Do not offer the parts of your body to sin, as instruments of wickedness, but rather offer yourselves to God, as those who have been brought from death to life; and offer the parts of your body to him as instruments of righteousness. For sin shall not be your master, because you are not under law, but under grace."

The second step to living honestly follows naturally from Paul's advice:

Second: *Avoid doing things that will require a lie to cover up.*

If you continue to sin when you know it's wrong, eventually you'll have to lie to keep others from finding out. If you cheat on a test, you'll be tempted to lie when you're asked how you got such an unusually good grade. If you disobey your parents, you'll have to invent many different lies to cover your tracks. If you say something unkind about someone, and they hear about it, what are you going to say when they confront you?

Any time you try to hide what you're doing, you're setting yourself up to lie. But if you live openly, avoiding secret sins, your life will demonstrate the kind of integrity that will cause others to trust you.

Have you made a mistake? Did you give in to temptation? Admit it right away. The pain or punishment you may suffer is small compared to the penalty you'll pay for trying to cover it with a lie.

Daniel provides a good example of honest living. Even his enemies were confounded by his integrity. They followed him around trying to find some secret in his life that they could use to destroy him. They searched with determination for a long time—and found nothing that he was doing wrong. Finally, they had to trick the king into making a new law against praying in order to trap Daniel. Even so, he continued to pray—openly, not trying to cover anything up—because he knew it was right.

You know the rest of that story (if not, read it in Daniel 6). The penalty for breaking the king's new law was death in the lions' den. When Daniel's enemies reported Daniel, the king realized that he'd been tricked. With great sadness, he agreed to stick to his word; he had Daniel thrown into the lions' den. But God came to Daniel's rescue and closed the lion's mouths. When Daniel emerged unhurt the next day, it was his deceitful enemies who had to face the lions for lying.

I have often asked myself: How would I fare if enemies spied on me day and night to find some flaw? Would they find me as clean as Daniel? "They could find no corruption in him, because he was trustworthy and neither corrupt nor negligent" (Daniel 6:4).

How to Develop Personal Integrity

I'm afraid there have been many times in my life when I'd have ended up as kitty litter in a lion's den if anyone had scrutinized the way I was living. How about you? If you're in the same boat as me, don't despair. Instead, make it your goal to trust in God's power to strive toward a holy and blameless life.

Learn to Be Dependable

Notice that in the verse I quoted two paragraphs ago, Daniel's enemies found that he was neither corrupt *nor* negligent. Unlike many modern politicians (Daniel was a politician), Daniel kept his promises. That was not a quality that he suddenly developed in order to keep his political office. It was a policy he had established long before—as a teenager. As a boy, Daniel had made a commitment to God not to defile himself with certain foods that he had been taught were dishonoring to God. Still a teenager, he had been captured by an enemy army, marched far away to an alien land, and told to eat those unsuitable foods. He refused; he risked his life to keep the promise he had made to God.

Personal integrity is not only the goal of a Christian —it is also a requirement for good relationships. When you discover a friendship that has soured, you will often also discover that someone has broken his or her word.

When you make a promise to someone, keep it.

If you tell your parents that you're going to be home at eleven, be home at eleven. It's easy to rationalize that a couple of minutes won't make any difference, or to assume that they will understand. When you don't keep your word, your friends and family stop trusting you. If you've promised to meet a friend or do a chore, don't fail to keep your promise. See it through.

"But I couldn't help it," you say. "I had every intention of doing what I said, but circumstances prevented me. It was beyond my control." Sometimes that's true. And in that case, you need to let people know (*beforehand*) that you have made every effort to keep your word. And, incidentally, that's why you need to be very careful before you make promises that you *will* be able to carry them out. Even if there were reasons you couldn't keep your word, people will still be disappointed in you. If you promise to accompany a friend to a game, don't keep your fingers crossed, thinking that you'll keep that promise only if no better offer comes along. It would be better not to make the promise in the first place.

Few things are more tempting than to spread a juicy story when someone tells us something in confidence and we agree not to tell. Keep your word. With few exceptions, *when you promise to keep a secret, keep it.* Nothing will cause you to lose more friends than betraying their confidence. If you can be trusted, your peers will seek you out for advice because so few people can be trusted with confidential information. Being able to keep a confidence enables your friends to take off their mask without fear. Keep your word.

The only exception to this rule is when your friend's life or personal welfare might be endangered by your silence. For example, if a friend tells you he is considering suicide, you must not keep that information to yourself. Your friend will probably be angry with you for a while, but it's much better to have an angry friend than a dead one.

How to Develop Personal Integrity

CHAPTER

10

PREPARING
FOR THE
FUTURE

Ever heard of the myth dragons?

You have now.

Whether you're into science fiction and fantasy or not, there are seven myths that stand like dragons at the gate to your future. You may not think of yourself as a dragonslayer, but like it or not you'd better find some way to kill these dragons because, unless you do, their fiery breath can destroy you.

What are the myth dragons? We've talked a lot in this book so far about lies, and that's just what the myth dragons are—the lies of Satan. That's why they can only be killed with the sword of truth. In this chapter, I'll give you that sword. But I can't slay the dragons for you.

That part's up to you.

Myth Dragon #1

"It doesn't matter how I live now—I can always make it right when I'm older."

Sword #1: "Be very careful, then, how you live—not as unwise but as wise, making the most of every opportunity, because the days are evil" (Ephesians 5:15–16).

One of the biggest lies in the universe goes like this: "I'll mess around while I'm in high school, and then when I get out then I'll settle down and think about my future." I'm not saying, necessarily, that anyone who says those words is a liar—it's the *idea* that is a lie.

I'm sure you've heard the saying, "I'll cross that bridge when I come to it." No, you won't. Why? Because, even though you may not know it, you're already on the bridge.

Does the high-school student who claims she'll settle down after graduating really believe that when her fingers touch that diploma she can suddenly become a different person? She may believe it, but it isn't going to happen. The patterns she has set in the past four years of her life can't be changed overnight. Even if she very badly wants to change, her past may stand in the way. For example: If she wants to go to law school but has waited until graduation to get serious about it, she may find it difficult to even get into a good college. One look at her poor grades will convince the admissions officer that she isn't law-school material.

At the request of a high-school counselor, I talked with a young man who had just been suspended for drinking. He told me about the difficult time he was having at home and school. "It's too much for me, man," he concluded. "I'm just going to drink and party until people get off my case and I can get a little space. Then I'll settle down."

I can still see the look on his face when, as I explained it to him, he realized that the patterns he had established in high school would quickly slam the doors to all opportunity for the future. At sixteen he had developed a dependence on alcohol, a record of poor grades, and a self-destructive pattern of behavior. Unless he was willing to make some changes in his life now, his future looked pretty dim.

In high school I had an interesting and completely ineffective way of doing homework. Big assignments such as term papers didn't have to be done for weeks, so whenever I was given an assignment like that I would forget about it until just before it was due. It never dawned on me to take the time to do it right. I guess I just thought the distant due date was established so that I could watch more TV. Many times I would start work on these huge assignments the night before they were due. I would dig out my dear friend the *Encyclopedia Britannica* and begin to copy. Every three or four sentences,

I would put in a new word or leave one out that was too big to understand.

Unfortunately, my teachers must have had read every encyclopedia in the world, because I couldn't fool them. They realized that if they could read what I had written, and if it made sense, then it must have come from the encyclopedia, because I certainly had never written anything that made sense on my own.

I reached the bottom when I was supposed to write a paper on the Lewis and Clark Expedition. I waited even longer than usual. In fact, the morning it was due, I hadn't even started. Centered at the top of a single sheet of paper, I wrote "Lewis and Clark Expedition." Beneath that I wrote, "See Exploration—*Encyclopedia Britannica*." I figured that rather than going to the trouble of copying all that material only to receive a failing grade, the teacher might as well read the encyclopedia on her own and then fail me.

When I look back on the grades I received because of those habits, I'm both ashamed and thankful. I'm ashamed that I developed those terrible shortcut habits and wasted so much of my life, but I'm thankful that this pattern was broken by someone who helped me see where I was headed.

Early in my college years, a professor I respected called me into his office. "What do you want to do with your life?" he asked. I told him my life's dreams. Then he shocked me. "I don't believe you," he said.

"Why?" I asked, angry and embarrassed.

I'll never forget his answer. "I don't believe you because nothing you're doing right now will bring you any closer to those goals. If you really wanted to see those dreams come true, you'd be working toward them now." Instead, I was working toward becoming a lazy bum. To this day, I'm grateful for that confrontation. Before I left his office, he kindly showed me how my study habits today would make a big difference in the opportunities that would be available to me tomorrow.

You won't be able to "cross that bridge when you come to it" until you realize that what you are doing right now will have a profound effect on your future.

It's important not to focus on a list of traditional no-no's and neglect other habits that affect your future. I grew up believing that if you didn't smoke, dance, drink, or chew, you were a pretty good person. In fact, when I met a person who didn't do that particular list of nasties, I was pretty sure that person must be a Christian.

Now, of course, I realize that it's a relationship with Christ that makes one a Christian. That hit me like a brick one day when I was sitting on the porch and my dog Ralph walked by. Ralph didn't smoke, drink, dance, or chew, and we never let him run around with dogs that were involved in those kinds of things. If those were the only things that determined whether you were a Christian, then Ralph was a better Christian than most people I knew. But Ralph had other disgusting habits too numerous and gross to mention.

Other bad habits not on the traditional hit list include spending hours in front of the television, overeating, an uncontrolled temper, lying, and on and on. For some of us, television-watching is our primary activity during our waking hours. Life is just too short to spend it watching material that can't help you live. We laugh at the term "couch potato," but the fact is that young people in this country spend an average of over five hours a day watching television. Over a period of fifty years, that amounts to *over fifteen years of your life, every waking hour* —wasted time that could have been spent living instead of vegetating.

What are the habits in your life that need to be expelled? How can they be replaced with new habits that will enable you to grow in Christ and work toward your goals?

Maybe you're saying, "Ken, you can't just start a good habit from scratch."

Yes, you can. In fact, that's just how all habits get started. When I was about thirteen, one of my cousins invited me out behind the barn to try something new. He had stolen a package of cigarettes and was going to give me the privilege of learning to smoke. This was thrilling. Now I could be cool like all the actors I had seen on television. (Back then *everybody* on TV smoked cigarettes, even Lassie and Mr. Ed.) The fact that my parents disapproved made it even more of an adventure.

For a while I just pulled the smoke into my mouth and blew it back out. Then he told me that real men inhaled the smoke. "Do you want to be a real man?" he asked. Well, I preferred being a real man over the next best alternative, so I pulled the biggest cloud of smoke I could into my mouth and then, at his signal, I took a deep breath.

When that cigarette smoke came in contact with my pink healthy lung tissue, my whole body heaved in desperation to get it out of there. Tears streamed from my eyes, and saliva came from everywhere. My body turned on all the hoses to try to get rid of that smoke. I coughed uncontrollably and couldn't catch my breath. Then I turned to my cousin and threw up.

But do you know what? As horrible as that felt and tasted, I did it again (although my cousin stood a little farther away the next time). And then again. Soon it was a habit that plagued me well into my adult life.

If you have never smoked, used drugs, drunk liquor,

cheated on a test, or dabbled in any of the other nasty little habits that can eat away at your health and your life, you are to be envied. Use that energy and willpower to develop good habits that will lengthen your life and pave the way to your future.

If you're already strangled by bad habits, I encourage you to do what I have had to do many times in my life. Admit your weakness to God and ask him to deliver you from that bondage. There's no freedom in being trapped by some habit that rules your life.

I remember being teased by one of my high-school friends for not attending a drinking party. I felt like an outsider —until one day I heard that same friend bragging about his experience the night before. "I must have thrown up six or seven times," he boasted. "I drank most of the six-pack and then passed out. Gary said I kept calling for my mommy." His circle of admiring friends was laughing as he concluded, "Boy, did we have a great time. I have a headache that could kill an elephant."

And that's when I realized that if having a good time is throwing up and getting a splitting headache, then I should sneak outside, stick my finger down my throat, and ram my head against a brick wall. After all, that would be cheaper than buying all that booze.

I kept track of my high-school friend who boasted to his friends that day about his drinking prowess. He's been in and out of alcoholic treatment centers since he was twenty. That was a future he chose for himself, whether he knew it or not, when he developed a drinking habit at fifteen.

Now is the time to ask Christ to help you dump that bad habit and get hooked on a good one.

Myth Dragon #2

"I am invincible. Nothing bad can happen to me."

Sword #2: "He is not prepared to live, who is not prepared to die."

You can set yourself up for tremendous disappointment and personal danger by believing you are invincible. Two weeks ago they removed the body of a teenage boy from the mountains near my home. He had been climbing in an area that was posted as extremely dangerous. His friends had tried to get him to come down, but he wouldn't. Just before he fell, he yelled down to them. "Don't worry, nothing can happen to me." What was he thinking—that he was too young to die?

Every year, thousands of girls face the reality of pregnancy because they thought that those kinds of things only happened to other people.

You are *not* invincible! Believing that you are can destroy your life. Most people who take unnecessary risks aren't doing it because they're brave—they're doing it because they don't believe that anything bad could happen to them at all. There's nothing brave in that—only foolish. Our decisions *do* have consequences. This is one myth dragon that is deadly. You must kill it, because if you don't it can kill you.

I was reminded of my own immortality just last month when I attended the funeral of a friend only a few years older than I. Yesterday, the ten-year-old son of another friend was killed riding his bicycle. We don't like to think about tragedies like these, because they remind us that we will also die someday. But there is an advantage in not pretending that you're going to live forever—it makes you want to live each day to the fullest.

Preparing for the Future

Someday, you will die. That's not some morbid truth that only applies to you. It applies to everyone. Every now and then I take a quiet walk through a cemetery. As I look at each marker, I'm reminded that those people probably thought they would live forever. When I leave, I am energized and renewed by the realization that time is precious, and I want to make the best of every minute God has allotted me. I also find myself rejoicing that, for those who have trusted Christ, that cemetery is not the end. It's the beginning of eternal life.

So don't believe the myth that you are invincible just because you are young. Live as though you were born yesterday and you have just this one day to give your best for God.

Myth Dragon #3

"Time is on my side."

Sword #3: "Remember your Creator in the days of your youth, before the days of trouble come and the years approach when you will say, 'I find no pleasure in them'" (Ecclesiastes 12:1).

Not only is time precious because it's limited in quantity; it's also precious because it goes by so *quickly*. When you're young, it's hard to see how fast time flies. But think for a minute—remember how long summer vacations seemed when you were very young? Now it seems like they just get started and you have to go back to school. In a few more years, a whole year will seem to take about the same time that a summer vacation takes now.

When you were in first grade, did you look at those old people in junior high and high school and think how ancient they were? Then you blinked your eyes, and now you're an ancient upperclassman. First graders think you're a fossil.

You probably look at people my age (early forties) and think we must have one foot in the grave. Well, don't blink again, because when you open your eyes you'll be just like me —and you'll wonder how the time went by so fast.

That's why it's so dangerous to think you have all kinds of time to really get serious about God. Time is *not* on your side. The Bible encourages you, in the verse I quoted above, to consider your Creator now while you're young. Christianity isn't for old people—it's for all people. These years can be the best years of your life—*if* you shake off the myth that you have plenty of time.

I've heard hundreds of adults express great regret that they didn't live for Christ during their youth. They were going to do it tomorrow, but tomorrow never came. Let him begin to shape your life *now,* so that your future and your forever will be as bright as he wanted them to be.

Only one life—'twill soon be past.
Only what's done for Christ will last.

Myth Dragon #4

"I'll just die if I have to wait."

Sword #4: "Good things come to those who wait."

Derek couldn't wait to own the convertible he saw for sale. It was his dream car. He bought it even though he couldn't afford to maintain it, or even to make the payments. By November, the car was repossessed. Instead of being able to start college as he had planned, Derek was broke and working at a hamburger stand.

I hear these expressions of impatience all the time:
I can't wait to get married.
I can't wait to graduate.

I can't wait to get my driver's license.

I can't wait to leave home.

I can't wait to turn twenty-one.

It's okay to look forward to each of those events in your life. But the truth is, you *can* wait, and it won't kill or maim you. The student who really believes that he can't wait to graduate so that he can gain his independence might just decide to rush things by dropping out of school. He'll soon discover he should have waited. The couple who can't wait to get married so that they can share their love in intercourse might just decide to go ahead and share their bodies with each other anyway, married or not—and they'll discover that not waiting brings on a new set of problems they're not prepared to face.

Learn to wait. It's a skill you'll definitely need for the future.

There is value in waiting; it can give you a new perspective that can make a big difference in your life. My daughter Traci never had any money because every time she got any she spent it on something she couldn't wait to have. The garage began to fill up with things she didn't need or use. I taught her to wait before buying. The system we used is the same one I discussed in chapter 7: When she felt she just *had* to have something, she would write it on a piece of paper and wait thirty days. Usually, long before the thirty days was up, she discovered that the item she just "couldn't wait" to have, she no longer wanted. As a result, she had the money for the things she really needed.

Waiting can keep you from making mistakes; it builds character; and it's the beginning of real maturity. Some people never learn this lesson. In Tennessee, two convicts dug under a fence and escaped to freedom. Within hours they were recaptured and returned to prison, where they both had several years added to their sentence for their escape attempt. Strangely enough, at the time they dug under the fence, one of the men had only thirty days left on his sentence. When he was asked why he would risk extra years on his sentence when he could have been out in thirty days, he simply replied, "I couldn't wait."

Remember: You can't force the future to come to you by refusing to wait. But by *not* waiting, you can force changes that will ruin your future forever. Don't be afraid to wait.

Myth Dragon #5

"Pain is bad, and I must avoid it at all costs."

Sword #5: "Consider it pure joy, my brothers, whenever you face trials of many kinds, because you know that the testing of your faith develops perseverance. Perseverance must finish its work so that you may be mature and complete, not lacking anything" (James 1:2–4).

"In this you greatly rejoice, though now for a little while you may have had to suffer grief in all kinds of trials. These have come so that your faith—of greater worth than gold, which perishes even though refined by fire—may be proved genuine and may result in praise, glory and honor when Jesus Christ is revealed" (1 Peter 1:6–7).

This myth dragon—that pain is bad and must be avoided at all costs—will cause you to set unworthy goals. Pain isn't bad. It's simply a fact of life. And often it's the price you must pay to reach a worthy goal. If you want to know the truth, for instance, you must go through the struggle of study and research to discover the truth. If you want to have a relationship with another person, you must go through the pain of

Preparing for the Future

vulnerability and confrontation in the building of that relationship. If you want to learn to fly an airplane, or water-ski, or play football, there will always be a price to pay.

If you believe the myth that life is only good when there is no pain, you'll always be mad at God. Whenever something happens to disturb your comfort, you'll cry out, "Why me, God? What did I do to deserve this?"

In John 16:33, Jesus told his disciples that as long as they lived in this world they would experience hardship and temptation: "I have told you these things, so that in me you may have peace. In this world you will have trouble. But take heart! I have overcome the world."

He never promised that life would be easy. So, if you experience difficulty and pain in your life, it's not because God is out to get you. It's because you are *alive*! The only people on this earth who have no pain are those who are dead or who are locked in a little padded room, yelling, "I feel no pain! I feel no pain!"

You can't climb a mountain or grow in your relationship with Christ or accomplish anything of value unless you are willing to pay a price. You can choose to go through life simply trying to avoid pain and accomplishing nothing, or you can set delight in the future and prepare to pay the price to reach those worthy goals.

Myth Dragon #6

"Romance will solve all my problems."

Sword #6: "A new command I give you: Love one another. As I have loved you, so you must love one another. By this all men will know that you are my disciples, if you love one another" (John 13:34–35).

"And now these three remain: faith, hope and love. But the greatest of these is love" (1 Corinthians 13:13).

Movies, records, and television reinforce with a vengeance the myth that romance solves all problems. Lonely and desperate men have their lives turned around in less than an hour when they find an adoring woman to give them love. Women facing unbelievable odds are saved when a knight in shining armor sweeps them off their feet.

But the truth is that romantic love will not solve your problems. As beautiful and fulfilling as it is to be loved, God (in the verses I quoted above) clearly taught us that the kind of love that was most powerful and most likely to give meaning and purpose to your life is different. It is not the kind of love you *get*; rather, it is the kind of love you *give*. In 1 Corinthians 13:4–13, that love is described. Here's part of that description (you'll want to read the rest, too):

> Love is patient, love is kind. It does not envy, it does not boast, it is not proud. It is not rude, it is not self-seeking, it is not easily angered, it keeps no record of wrongs. Love does not delight in evil but rejoices with the truth. It always protects, always trusts, always hopes, always perseveres. Love never fails.
>
> *1 Corinthians 13:4–8a*

If you expect all your problems to go away when you find someone to love you, you're setting yourself up for tremendous disappointment. In fact, you just might doom yourself to being unsuccessful in love because you'll place such high demands on your relationship and on the person who falls in love with you; you'll be asking that person to make you whole, something only God can do. But if you accept the fact that God's love is sufficient for all your needs and you set as a goal for your life sharing that love with others, you will be much better prepared for the realities of the future.

Preparing for the Future

Myth Dragon #7

"God is just a theory or theology or something."

Sword #7: "For God so loved the world that he gave his one and only Son, that whoever believes in him shall not perish but have eternal life" (John 3:16).

"For we do not have a high priest who is unable to sympathize with our weaknesses, but we have one who has been tempted in every way, just as we are—yet was without sin" (Hebrews 4:15).

God is a person who loved you enough to sacrifice his own Son so that you might live. He sent Jesus so that you personally could know forgiveness and abundant life. You can kill the myth that God is just a theory by trusting him for the forgiveness of your sins and for the everyday guidance that will allow you to face the future with confidence.

My children always hated the fun house at the fair because they didn't know what was in there. They would agree to go only if I would hold their hand and lead them through. They knew that *I* knew what was in there, and they trusted me because I loved them.

A youth worker asked his little daughter if she wanted to go for a ride. Yes, she *loved* going for car rides with her daddy—until they turned in to the ride-through car wash. She had been through the car wash before, and the sound of the blasting water and the sight of the brushes engulfing the car had scared her to death. "Let's stop at McDonald's and then go to the zoo," she begged, trying to avoid this terrible experience. But it didn't work, and when the car was pulled into the spray of water, she jumped onto her dad's lap, held her face very close to his, and looked him directly in the eyes. "Talk to me, Daddy," she pleaded. He talked to her all the way through the car wash. She discovered that it wasn't so scary after all, as long as she was looking right into her father's eyes and he continued to talk to her.

God offers that same guidance to you; he wants you to recognize him as the same kind of loving father. Focus your attention on him. Let him talk to you. He knows the future, he loves you, and he is willing to lead you every step of the way.

Now that we've discussed these myth dragons, you must realize that preparing for the future begins today. If you believe some of these myths, you'll wait until it's too late. Are you letting any of these myths stand at the gate of your future, blocking your entrance to the best options, the best choices? If so, what steps will you take to eliminate their influence in your life?

Develop a plan to kill each of these dragons. When they're all dead, you'll be ready to move toward the future with confidence.

Preparing for the Future

CHAPTER

11

WALKING
WITH GOD

As important as it is to prepare for the future, there's nothing you can do to actually *control* the future. That's not your job. There isn't a person reading this book who can guarantee even the next few minutes of his life. The future is in the hands of God.

Fortunately, he isn't the kind of God who takes pleasure in watching you stumble around in the dark. He created you for a purpose; he gave you incredible potential. And he wants to see you accomplish that purpose and live up to that potential. To make those things possible, he is available every day to surround you in love, forgive your sin, and show you how to live each day. Do you want to know God in that way? Then the next move is yours.

Many people believe that when they place their faith in Christ, that's the end of it—that's all they need to do. Really, that's just the beginning. God knows all about you—now he wants you to get to know him. So how do you go about getting to know God? That's what this chapter is about.

Talk to God

One morning, not long after Diane and I were married, I saw her wedding ring lying on the bathroom sink. I thought it would be great fun to make her think it was lost, so I hid the ring.

That evening, Diane asked me if I had seen her ring. I wasn't ready for the joke to be over yet, so I said no.

Late at night, I woke up to the sound of uncontrollable sobbing. "What's wrong?" I mumbled, still half asleep.

"Nothing," she replied. Now I was wide awake. How was it possible to be crying uncontrollably in the middle of the night over nothing? After a great deal of probing, she finally blurted out, "I've lost my wedding ring."

What a relief! This was something I could solve immediately. "I have your ring," I confessed, thinking she would hug me in relief and I could go back to sleep.

The embrace never came. "What?" she growled.

"I took your ring as a joke," I said. "I know just where it is, so you can go to sleep." It was dark, so I didn't see her fist coming—but I did feel it land. In twenty years of marriage, that was the only time she ever hit me. It was also the last time I ever took her wedding ring.

We talked late into the night about trust and the importance of communication. First, of course, I should have immediately confessed that I took the ring as soon as she asked me whether I'd seen it. Second, she should have told me then that she thought she'd lost it and that she was heartbroken. It cost me a black eye, but we learned the importance of talking to each other that night.

In relationships, silence isn't golden—it's deadly.

If you don't believe that statement, just go to school for a day without speaking to your friends. And I guarantee that one hour of silence will convince your date that he or she has lizard's breath. Yet sometimes we go weeks without talking to the one who loves us most, and then we wonder why we don't feel close to him. Let's look at some of the misconceptions that keep us from talking to God. Then let's tear them down forever.

Misconception 1: *Prayer is limited to asking God for something.*

You would be deeply hurt if someone you loved never spoke to you unless he wanted something. God does want you to ask him for the things you need—but prayer is much more than that. It's a conversation between two people who love each other. In this case, one of those people is God. But it won't be much of a conversation if you don't *talk* to him about the things that are important to you, about your hopes and dreams and fears and disappointments. He wants to hear your expressions of love for him and your thanks for the many things he has given you. Don't wait until you need something to talk to God. He wants to talk with you every day.

Misconception 2: *Prayer is a foreign language.*

I have talked to teenagers who are afraid to pray; they're afraid they'll use the wrong words. They have always heard prayers that sounded like this:

"O Lord, hearest the prayer of thy servant. Wouldest thou helpest me to be whatest thou wantest me to be, dear God, and scattereth abroad thy abundant mercies upon my heart. Showeth me thy will, O Lord, and giveth me thy strength for the day."

If Jesus walked up to your house today, he wouldn't talk like most prayers you hear. He didn't even talk like that during the days he walked the earth. It's odd, when you think about it: Somehow we have come to believe–just because an English translation of the Bible called the King James Version (released in the year 1611!) was written in that kind of language—that prayers are more spiritually correct if they are prayed in seventeenth-century English. The language used in the King James Bible wasn't spoken in Jesus' time. In fact, they didn't speak English at all. Jesus and his friends spoke Greek and Aramaic.

If you feel more comfortable praying that way, that's okay. But you don't have to. You can talk to God the same way you talk to a respected friend.

And regardless of what language you pray in, don't worry about God being able to understand you. Even when you have trouble expressing yourself, God knows what you are trying to say.

> We do not know what we ought to pray for, but the Spirit himself intercedes for us with groans that words cannot express. And he who searches our hearts knows the mind of the Spirit, because the Spirit intercedes for the saints in accordance with God's will.   *Romans 8:26–27*

Misconception 3: *God only wants to hear good things.*
One boy told me he was afraid to confess his sins to God because he was afraid that God would be so angry at him when he heard what the boy had done that God would do something horrible as punishment. It took me a while to convince him that God would not be surprised at his confession. Can you imagine the following scene?

Boy: O God, forgive me for cursing at my teacher.

God: (Slapping his forehead in surprise) Oh no! Freak me out! You *swore* at your teacher? What am I going to do now?

What a ridiculous scenario. God knows about your sins even as you *think* them. He wants you to confess to him because he wants to continue his forgiveness, to wipe the slate clean, and give you the power to go forward—not so he can find out what you've done.

> If we confess our sins, he is faithful and just, and will forgive us our sins and purify us from all unrighteousness. If we claim we have not sinned, we make him out to be a liar and his word has no place in our lives.   *1 John 1:9–10*

When you don't make a habit of confessing your sins to God and asking his forgiveness, you begin to build a wall between you and him. Each time you avoid him, you put another brick in the wall. But understand this: *You're* the one building the wall, not God. Confession tears the wall down.

So don't be afraid to talk openly to God about your sins

and failures. You aren't telling him something he doesn't already know; it's for *your* benefit that he wants you to confess them. And remember that it's okay to express disappointment and anger to God. David told God that his bones felt like dust. When he was hanging on the cross, Jesus cried out in anguish, "My God, my God, why have you forsaken me?" You can feel free to be open and honest with God.

Misconception 4: *You should always kneel and close your eyes when you pray.*

Kneeling and closing your eyes when you pray is a great way to show respect to God and block out distractions. Even so, there's no special posture required for prayer. I often shout my prayers as I run around a lake near my home. The other joggers give me lots of room to run. Some of them probably think I'm a nut case—so what? I really don't care. As I run, I think, and many of the things I think about I want to talk to God about. Why should I wait until I get home and kneel?

Any place is a good place to talk to God. When the engine failed in my airplane, I didn't kneel or close my eyes. I just whispered, "Please pay attention, Jesus."

The Bible says that we should pray continually:

> Be joyful always; pray continually; give thanks in all circumstances, for this is God's will for you in Christ Jesus.
> *1 Thessalonians 5:16–18*

Be aware of God's presence; talk to him all day long. In the morning, silently thank him for the sunrise. Before you read your devotions, ask him to show you what he wants for the day. On the way to school, ask him to help you remember what you have studied for that important test. If you do poorly in the test, don't be afraid to tell him that you're disappointed. If you could see Jesus by your side all day, you would talk to him constantly. Well, he's really there—and he would like to talk with you.

Today, while driving home from a speaking engagement, I asked God to help me face a temptation that has been plaguing me the past few days. I didn't say a word out loud, but I know that God heard a very specific prayer—and by praying it, by talking to God, I found that I felt very close to him. You'll be amazed how continual prayer will make you aware of God's presence. I think that's one of the reasons he asks us to pray all the time. He created us to have a relationship with him, and our constant contact makes him very happy. It will also make you love him more.

- Thank him every day—whenever you think of it.
- Confidently ask him for the things you need.
- Pray for your friends who need to know him.
- Pray for friends who have needs.
- Ask him to show you what to do in difficult situations.
- Praise him for who he is.
- Ask him to help you live for him.
- Tell him your dreams.
- Tell him of your disappointments.

Do all of the above—in your own language, any time and any place, all the time.

Listen as God Talks to You

How does God talk to you? How do you learn about him? Through the Bible. As you develop a relationship with a friend, you ask questions, talk, listen—things that help you learn more about this person you want a relationship with. If you want a relationship with God, you do the same thing— except that in this case, you learn more about him and what he wants for your life by reading the Bible.

Walking with God

I Don't Remember Dropping the Skunk, But . . .

Those who sincerely search the Scriptures are amazed to find comfort and guidance as well as a gripping (and humbling) awareness of their own sin. How does that happen? It happens because God's Word is powerful; as you read it, the Holy Spirit will direct the words you're reading toward your own personal needs. It isn't a dead book. It is, in fact, a book like no other.

> I have hidden your word in my heart that I might not sin against you. *Psalm 119:11*

> Your word is a lamp to my feet and a light for my path. *Psalm 119:105*

> For the word of God is living and active. Sharper than any double-edged sword, it penetrates even to dividing soul and spirit, joints and marrow; it judges the thoughts and attitudes of the heart. *Hebrews 4:12*

> All Scripture is God-breathed and is useful for teaching, rebuking, correcting and training in righteousness, so that the man of God may be thoroughly equipped for every good work. *2 Timothy 3:16–17*

Years ago someone wrote in my Bible, "This book will keep you from sin, or sin will keep you from this book." And that's true. It's not a magic formula—a verse a day doesn't keep the devil away. But neglecting to study the Bible will eventually affect your relationship with the Lord. Absence doesn't make the heart grow fonder; it makes you quickly forget him. No one enjoys being around someone who never listens. Let God get a word in edgewise. Give your relationship with him a chance to grow by letting him talk to you through his Word.

Here are some suggestions to help you get the most out of the Bible:

First, discipline yourself to *read a little every day* —not just as a meaningless ritual, but as a means to allow God to speak to you. But don't just pick a few verses at random. That can lead you to misunderstand what God is trying to say to you.

There's a story about a man who would open his Bible every morning, close his eyes, and run his finger randomly down a page. When he opened his eyes, wherever his finger was pointing would be the verse he would live by for that day. One day he opened his eyes and his finger was pointing to Matthew 27:5: "Then he [Judas] went away and hanged himself." That was a pretty depressing verse to live by, so he concluded that there must have been some mistake. He flipped several pages and tried again. When he opened his eyes he was horrified to read, "Go thou and do likewise." Now somewhat shaken, he made one last attempt. His finger came to rest on John 13:27: "What you are about to do, do quickly!"

This approach to Bible reading is like overhearing part of a conversation and trying to guess what the people are talking about. Use a study guide to help you understand the total context of what you read. Your youth pastor or Sunday school teacher or parents can suggest a good study guide, but make sure they know you want one that will communicate effectively with you and that you don't need a college degree just to understand.

Try reading through the whole Bible in a year! That sounds like a lot, but actually it only adds up to a few minutes a day. *The NIV Student Bible,* published by Zondervan, not only shows you several plans for Bible reading, but also has lots of notes to help you understand what you're reading.

Second, *get involved in a Bible study with other kids your age.* Your Sunday school class, youth group, or confirmation

lass might work fine. If not, somewhere you can find a special
Bible study for your age group; ask your pastor or youth
pastor.

It's important to spend time with others where the exchange of ideas will sharpen your own understanding and Bible study skills and drive you to look closer at what the Bible says. And that brings us to the next important step in walking with God.

Spend Time with His Friends

The Bible is very clear about the importance of spending time with other believers. When I first trusted Christ, a well-meaning man put his arm around me and said, "Now all your problems are over." There have been several times since then when I've wanted to find that man.

The Christian life is not easy. If you've been a Christian for a while, you already know that. It is essential to have the support and encouragement of others who believe as you do, and to be able to offer them your support in return. The body of Christ (one of the terms the Bible uses to describe the church, meaning not just the local church but all followers of Christ everywhere) was designed by God to provide this kind of support.

Whether you find that support and friendship in your local church or in one of the nondenominational organizations like Young Life or Campus Life, the important thing is to get involved with other kids who believe in Christ. You'll be encouraged to find out that you aren't alone—there are millions of kids like you who take their faith seriously. Somehow, being with them, you are also with him. After all, Jesus said when two or more of you (believers) are gathered together, he will be there.

"For where two or three come together in my name, there am
with them."   *Matthew 18:20*

Talking to God, listening to him, and spending time
with his children are all steps you can take to walk with him
Take advantage of each of those steps. Walk with him every
day.

CHAPTER

12

KNOWING
THE WILL
OF GOD

Three Misconceptions About God's Will

There aren't many subjects that cause more confusion among Christians than knowing God's will. How do you know what God wants you to do? When you're trying to decide about college, or about becoming a pastor or a missionary, or about whether to say yes when someone asks you to marry him—*how do you know?*

One of the reasons there's so much confusion about it is that there are a lot of misconceptions about knowing God's will—even among the older Christians whom you might ask for advice. So let me explain some of those misconceptions for you. I hope that will help you avoid some of the frustration and even hostility toward God that often afflicts people who think they've missed God's will.

Misconception #1

God's will is always something I will hate.

As a teenager, I was afraid to trust God for fear that he would send me someplace where there were snakes, spiders, and people who eat other people. For sure it would be someplace I would hate.

I was afraid to pray to him about the girl I should marry; I was afraid that if I left it in his hands he'd surprise me with some withered-up prune.

This kind of thinking stems from the mistaken idea that God really doesn't understand us or care about us, that we are simply pawns he uses to accomplish his will. The truth is that he wants us to experience life in the most abundant way possible.

Don't get me wrong—this doesn't mean that God's will for us will be a cushy life with no pain. Some of the most contented people I know have followed God to places where there *are* snakes, spiders, and people who eat people. But they wouldn't trade the difficult lives they live for any of the comforts you and I enjoy. And we can learn a valuable truth from those people: That you won't find a more fulfilling life than the one you can live right in the center of God's will.

But how do you *get* there? How do you know what his will is? Hold on—I promise to help you answer those questions.

Misconception #2

I'm not good enough for God's will.

Another misconception that paralyzes many people is the belief that once you've done something against God's will, you'll forever have to settle for his second best. You've missed the boat, and even if you catch another boat later, you still won't be in the right places in the right times like you should have been. You'll probably be married to the wrong person, or you'll have gone to the wrong school, and yes, God can still use you—but not like he *could* have if you'd gotten it right in the first place.

I first heard this from someone counseling a teenage girl who had just had a baby outside of marriage. "Now you'll always have to settle for God's second best," he said. What a terrible thought! Although it's true that God's best design for mankind was messed up by sin (starting with Adam and Eve in the garden), it's also true that God made it possible for our sins to be forgiven through Jesus Christ. If, as the Bible says, we have *all* sinned, and if that sin bars us from knowing the "first-best" will of God forever, then why even try?

We try because God already *knows* that we have sinned, and he still says that we can experience his perfect will. If what that counselor said to that unwed mother was true, then what about his *own* sins? By his own statement he condemns himself to God's second best.

Will that young unmarried girl who had the baby face some consequences for her actions? Undoubtedly, as will the boy who fathered her child, and any of the rest of us who've been guilty of sexual immorality. But those consequences will not be God's punishment for her sins, nor will they mean banishment from his will. They will be the consequences that God was trying to save her from when he said, "Flee from sexual immorality ... but he who sins sexually sins against his own body" (1 Corinthians 6:18).

If you jump from a three-story building, you won't be able to run a marathon the next day. But I doubt very much that you would blame God. You would instinctively know that your broken bones, bruises, and sprains were simply a consequence of your action the previous day.

When a parent points toward a hot stove and says to his child, "Don't touch," he's trying to help his child avoid some painful consequences. If that child ignores the warning and touches the hot stove anyway, he will be burned. Is that burning the punishment that the parent hands out to his disobedient child? No. The parent was trying to help his child *avoid* being burned. The painful burn is simply the consequence of the child's action.

That young unmarried girl who had the baby may miss some of the opportunities available to her friends. That's not a punishment from God; it's a simple consequence of her actions. The beautiful thing about knowing Christ and experiencing his forgiveness is that God makes it possible for us to find and obey his will in spite of our sinful nature.

Many people mistakenly think that God's will is like a

raft. If you fall off, or get sidetracked on shore and miss the launch, the raft goes on without you and you'll never be able to catch up. In reality, God's will is more like the current in a river. You probably should have stepped into it yesterday—but if you didn't, the river's still there today, with the same current.

Did you miss some important opportunities because you didn't step in yesterday? Probably. But God continually seeks to restore the relationship you had with him. The Bible says, "When we confess our sins, he is faithful and just and will forgive us our sins and purify us from all unrighteousness" (1 John 1:9).

I believe that God's love and his will work the same way. Much like the current in the river, they are always there waiting. When you make up your mind to seek his forgiveness and obey his will, you slip back into the stream and are caught up in the current, the center of his will.

The reason I explain this at such length is that I have met so many kids who have totally given up because they believe that they have sinned too much to ever again be a part of what God wants. No matter what you have done, no matter how difficult your circumstances, God wants you back in the stream. He has a perfect will for you right where you are.

"But how do I find it?" you say, beating your fists against the wall. Just hang in there, because we need to clear up another misconception first.

Misconception #3

God's will is whatever I think it should be.

God's will is not simply a matter of opinion. Many people use this misconception to give credibility to their own ideas. A girlfriend once told me that God told her she shouldn't go with me anymore. How could I argue with her?

Knowing the Will of God

It would be like arguing with God. Basically, she was saying that God told her I wasn't good enough for her. (That did a lot for my self-image.) The simple truth was that she didn't want to go with me anymore, but to admit that would have made her responsible for her own decision.

We'll discuss below some of the characteristics of God's will and the ways in which we find out what it is. But please keep this in mind as we do so: God's will exists. It isn't something we make up; it isn't based simply on what we'd like it to be. It's God's will—not ours. It's more than an opinion —it's a plan. God's plan.

With those misconceptions out of the way, the door is now open to discovering the truth about God's will. Let's get to it.

The Main Sources for Knowing God's Will

You don't find God's will in your local newspaper's want ads, or an advice column, and usually not by asking your friends, either. Where do you find God's will? Let me tell you about three of the sources you'll use in your search.

The Bible: God's Will in Writing

Most of what you can know of God's will is found in his Word. The Bible tells you specifically what your relationship with God was meant to be, how you should treat other people, and how you should make everyday decisions. For instance, there's no need to agonize over whether you should snub a friend who has wronged you, because the Bible clearly directs you to treat even your enemies with love.

Although the Bible doesn't speak directly to every situation you'll face, the guidelines are sufficient to point you to the right action. When you face daily decisions, and even the big, long-term decisions like the choice of a career, you'll search in vain for a specific answer that tells you, for instance, whether to be a doctor or a teacher. Instead, God's guidance in his Word comes in the form of principles that we apply to our specific situations.

Let's take the question: Whom should you marry? Does God have one person picked out for you and assign you the job of finding out who this mystery person is? Or does he want you to follow the guidelines set up in Scripture for choosing a mate and then trust him to lead you to the right kind of person?

Don't expect a voice to come from heaven directing you to a specific course of action in every little daily choice you make. God has already given us that "voice from heaven." It's the Bible. Learn what it says about the way God wants us to live, and then use your brain to apply those principles to the daily decisions you make.

Natural Law Is God's Will

I'm always amazed when I meet Christians who mistakenly believe that they are exempt from this aspect of God's will. Sometimes they seem to expect God's will to be contrary to the natural laws that he established.

It just doesn't work that way. There's no need to wonder if it's God's will that you pass an exam if you haven't studied for the exam—you probably won't pass it anyway, God's will or not. Similarly, don't intentionally mistreat your body, arguing that you'll die when it's God's will for you to die. God is the one who created your body in such a way that, if you mistreat it, you're likely to die sooner than if you treat it well.

Take a sharp curve at 100 mph, and the law of gravity

Knowing the Will of God

(God's will) will cause your car to leave the road. Don't enter a sharp curve at 100 mph thinking that, because you're a Christian, you're exempt from his natural laws. If a Christian and a non-Christian jump from the Empire State Building at the same time, they'll both hit the ground at the same time. And just as hard.

The natural laws that govern this universe are universal. Why do I bring this up? Because it's important that, as you make daily decisions concerning God's will, you take his natural law into consideration. When God put the laws that govern this world in place, they became part of his will.

The Holy Spirit Reveals God's Will

"But the Counselor, the Holy Spirit, whom the Father will send in my name, will teach you all things and will remind you of everything I have said to you" (John 14:26).

"But when he, the Spirit of truth, comes, he will guide you into all truth. He will not speak on his own; he will speak only what he hears, and he will tell you what is yet to come. He will bring glory to me by taking what is mine and making it known to you" (John 16:13–14).

God also reveals his will as the Holy Spirit touches your heart and mind to move you to action. But, because the Holy Spirit doesn't speak to us in any audible language, it's often hard to discern what he is saying—especially if you haven't tried hard to learn to recognize his leading. That's why it's always important to carefully examine what you believe the Holy Spirit is encouraging you to do, and to check it against the Bible for confirmation. If you don't, and if your mind and heart aren't firmly anchored in the truth of God's Word, you might fall into the trap of following other influences and motivations—the voices of your friends, or of our society, or

of your own desires, for instance—and attributing those to the Holy Spirit.

"I really feel the Holy Spirit leading me to go the Bible college and become a pastor," you might say, when it's possible that being a pastor really isn't your gift, isn't the best use of the talents God gave you. Maybe what you're really hearing is the voice of a well-meaning adult who has often told you that he'd love to see you become a pastor.

Learn to recognize the voice of the Holy Spirit, one of the most powerful ways God has of guiding us in our daily lives. And strengthen your ability to recognize his voice by studying the Bible's excellent guidelines for keeping your mind and heart in tune with God's will.

Paul's Formula for Knowing God's Will for Your Life

Enough preparation. Let's get on to the main question, the one teenagers ask most often: "How do I know what God wants for my life?"

Many people spend their lives almost paralyzed, trying to find the answer to this question. "Is this choice God's will or my own will?" they lament, trying to decide which college they should attend or which boy or girl they should date. Because they don't know what God wants them to do, they're afraid to do anything.

In the Old Testament, Gideon tested the will of God by laying a fleece on the ground. (A fleece is the woolly hide of a sheep.) You can read this story in Judges 6:36–40. "If you will save Israel by my hand as you have promised," Gideon said, "in the morning cover the fleece with dew and let the ground around it be dry." That was impossible, so Gideon knew that if it happened, it would be a sign from God.

Sure enough, in the morning the fleece was soaked and the ground around it was dry. But Gideon still wasn't sure. "Don't be angry with me," he said to God. "Let me make one more request. Allow me one more test with the fleece. This time make the *fleece* be dry and all the ground covered with dew." God patiently made it happen the next morning.

Many people still try the fleece method to find God's will. They set up elaborate tests for God to let them know which decision is the right one. They lay out so many fleeces that they forget which one belongs to which problem. Other times, they slant the test so that it will work out the way they want.

Once, before getting on a bus, I prayed silently: "Dear God, if you want me to talk to someone about your love today, please give me a sign."

I had just seated myself comfortably when a young businessman sat in the seat next to me. After a moment he began to cry uncontrollably. When he regained his composure, he turned to me and apologized, explaining that his life was a mess and that he had no hope of cleaning it up. "If only I knew God," he sighed. Then, looking directly at me, he asked, "Do you know God?"

Caught off guard, I quickly said another short prayer: "Dear God, is this a sign?" Of *course* God had led this man to me and wanted me to speak to him, but I was unwilling to follow up his leading. I thought of giving God a harder test like Gideon, just to make sure: "Dear God, if this is a sign, turn the bus driver into an armadillo."

How silly. The Bible is so full of directives to share God's love with those around us that, when the opportunity arises to do so, it's obviously God's will that we take advantage of that opportunity. A better prayer would have been, "Dear

God, give me the courage today to share my faith whenever the opportunity arises."

God doesn't try to hide his will from you. On the contrary, he wants you to know his will. That's why God gave us the Bible. Most of what he wants for you can be found within the pages of that book.

God also gave you a mind capable of reason. You can use common sense in making everyday decisions; similarly, much of finding God's will consists of using your mind to find the guidelines in the sources he provided.

Sometimes we want to escape from the responsibility of making personal decisions so we try to find answers in the Bible. The Bible gives very clear guidance on some questions. The man and woman contemplating an extramarital affair need not read far to discover God's condemnation of such activity. But in other areas the Bible has little or nothing to say. What does the Bible say about scuba diving? Nothing, of course. How then can Christians know whether it is God's will for them to take up scuba diving? Such persons would have to look for broad biblical principles of action. The Bible teaches that believers are responsible to use their time and money wisely, to take care of their physical bodies, to put the welfare of their families ahead of their own. One person might find that scuba diving takes too much time or costs too much for his limited budget. Others might find that the exhilaration that follows gives greater efficiency in their work for God and/or is a good activity to do with family members. Individual believers who honestly seek the mind of God in their lives must make such decisions after they "test everything; hold on to the [morally] good" (1 Thessalonians 5:21). (From: *Understanding Scripture* by A. Berkeley Mickelsen & Alvera M. Mickelsen, Ventura, California: Regal Books, 1982).

Finally, God gave you the Holy Spirit to work in your mind and heart to help you know what he wants. God never intended to make a guessing game out of questions like: Which school should I go to? Should I go out for the football team? Which class should I take? If your heart is right, and you know and follow God's Word, then most of the time your actions will be right.

How can you be *sure* of God's will? Paul answers that question very clearly in Romans 12:1-2. He doesn't suggest that you skin any sheep, start laying out fleeces, or ask him to change bus drivers into strange animals. Instead, he gives three steps that will help you know God's perfect will for your life.

Give God Your Body

The first step toward knowing the will of God is to give your body to God.

> Therefore, I urge you, brothers, in view of God's mercy, to offer your bodies as living sacrifices, holy and pleasing to God—this is your spiritual act of worship. *Romans 12:1*

That sounds so simple. Too bad it's one of the hardest things for a person to do. But it's impossible for you to know what God wants in your life unless your body belongs to him.

You've heard people talk about giving your life to Christ. Giving your *life* to Christ is easier to talk about—it's vague enough that it doesn't hurt much. But giving God your *body* is difficult because you care very much about your body, in very specific ways. When it's hungry, you feed it. When it hurts, you take care of it. One blemish on the end of your nose and you don't even want to show yourself in public.

Well, God wants it all. Hands, feet, lips, intellect, sex organs, eyes, even that blemish on the end of your nose. He wants it all offered to him as a living sacrifice.

Knowing the Will of God

Little children express the reality of this in a song they sing. The verses are:

Oh, be careful little hands what you do.
Oh, be careful little feet where you go.
Oh, be careful little eyes what you see.

And the chorus of this beautiful little song concludes:

For the Father up above is looking down in love,
So be careful little hands what you do.

In chapters 6 and 7 of Romans, Paul explains that we either give our hands and feet (and all the members of our body) to God to be used as instruments of righteousness or to Satan as instruments of sin. The first option leads to life—the other leads to death.

"What does this have to do with knowing God's will?" you may be asking. And here's the answer: Just think what would happen if you were to walk around school all day tomorrow singing to yourself, "Oh, be careful little lips what you say." I know it sounds crazy (it'll sound even crazier to the people around you, so be sure to sing it to yourself), but think about it for a moment. As you sang, you would be constantly aware that your lips belong to God. The first time you were tempted to hurt someone with cruel words, you would immediately remember that that is not what God would want you to do with those lips.

Let's face it—most days we never even *think* of God, let alone walk around with an awareness that our bodies belong to him. No wonder we have trouble knowing his will. If you give your body to God and constantly remind yourself that it belongs to him, you'll become more aware of what he wants. Have you unconditionally surrendered your body to the Savior? If not, now would be an excellent time. It's the first step toward knowing his will.

Give God Your Will

The second step is to give God your will. That means making up your mind that you want what he wants more than anything else. Instead of allowing your own desires or peer pressure to run your life, you allow God to run it.

How do you give your will to God? Paul puts it this way: "Do not conform any longer to the pattern of this world" (Romans 12:2). Another translation puts it even more clearly: "Don't let the world press you into its mold." If you're letting the mold of the world (pun intended) be the only influence in your decision making, you're going to have a terrible time figuring out what God wants you to do. If Jesus hadn't been totally committed to doing the will of his Father, we would be without hope today. But when all the pressures around him suggested that he should avoid the cross, he prayed, "Yet not as I will, but as you will" (Matthew 26:39). His decision to go to the cross wasn't an easy one to make, but he knew it was the right decision.

Who really owns your will? Is it your friends? Is it the culture around you? Or is it God? He wants nothing less than your total commitment to allow him to direct your life. If you're willing to make that commitment, he'll be able to show you what he wants. In fact, he'll help you to *want* what he wants and to do the things he wants you to do.

... for it is God who works in you to will and to act according to his good purpose. *Philippians 2:13*

Knowing the Will of God

Give God Your Mind

To know God's will, your commitment to avoid being pressured into the world's mold must be accompanied by a third step: Give God your mind. Paul puts it this way:

> Do not conform any longer to the pattern of this world, but be transformed by the renewing of your mind.   *Romans 12:2*

God wants your mind. You may say "Well, if he could see my report card, he wouldn't be so interested in my mind." That's not what he's talking about. Rather than focusing on the things of this world, God wants you to fill your mind with him.

That's why it's so important to read the Bible regularly. In fact, one of the best descriptions of how you transform your mind was written in the book of Psalms. See if you can find the two requirements for transforming your mind in these verses. I'll give you a hint: The first is something you avoid and the second is something you seek after.

> Blessed is the man who does not walk in the counsel of the wicked or stand in the way of sinners or sit in the seat of mockers. But his delight is in the law of the Lord, and on his law he meditates day and night.   *Psalm 1:1-3*

Watch what goes into your mind. The first requirement is in the first part of the verse. It suggests that you avoid the influence of evil people. Don't allow evil thinking to permeate your mind.

> The sinful mind is hostile to God. It does not submit to God's law, nor can it do so.   *Roman 8:7*

Genghis Khan swept across China and Mongolia, conquering everything in his path. Many of the cities he conquered had huge armies and were surrounded by immense walls, yet he managed to overcome them. When he was asked how he managed to get past the great protecting walls of those cities, he simply responded, "We bribed the gatekeeper." All he had to do was get past the person who guarded the city gate, and the city was easy pickings.

Your mind is like the city of your soul. If it can be conquered, your soul will crumble. Unfortunately, few people have a guard of any kind at the gate to their mind. They allow every thought, every idea, every image that comes along to enter their mind—and then wonder why they have a tough time knowing God's will.

If you want to transform your mind, you must decide that some influences will not be allowed to cloud your thinking. Then you must guard your mind from those influences. I think you know what I'm talking about. There are times when we should get up and leave the movie theater (or turn off the radio or the TV) because what is being communicated there is so contrary to the teaching of Christ, or so insulting to him.

If someone were insulting a person that you love, you would either leave the room or tell that speaker to shut up. Let's give Jesus Christ the same consideration. Let's refuse to allow destructive garbage that insults him to enter our mind. Why do we expose ourselves to such destructive material, anyway? Is it because we don't believe it will affect us? Nothing could be further from the truth.

A young man came to me because he was having a problem with his thought life. In his mind, he would undress every girl he met. He said he wanted to change all that. We talked for a while, and after a short prayer he left feeling better. Two days later I walked into the drug store to find him paging through magazines in the pornographic section of the magazine counter. No wonder he was having trouble with his thought life. If you allow garbage into your mind, your actions will be affected.

Imagine that as you are coming home from church one Sunday, you see a man standing on the railroad tracks. His clothing is torn, and he has been badly injured.

"What happened?" you ask him.

"I was hit by a train!" he cries. "Just about an hour ago. Please help me! I'm afraid it will happen again!"

What would you say to him? "If you don't want to get hit by a train—*get off the tracks*!"

I said basically the same thing to my young friend. If you want to clean up your thought life, stay away from the south end of the magazine counter. The psalmist's message is the same. Stay away from the "stinking thinking" that leads you further away from his will.

Renew your mind. The second requirement, then, is to replace stinking thinking with God's thinking. The psalmist puts it this way:

> But his delight is in the law of the Lord, and on his law he meditates day and night. He is like a tree planted by streams of water, which yields its fruit in season and whose leaf does not wither. Whatever he does prospers.   *Psalm 1:2–3*

The person who wants to be blessed by God immerses himself in God's Word and finds delight in discovering how God thinks and what he wants. That's why God can say:

> Delight yourself in the Lord and he will give you the desires of your heart.   *Psalm 37:4*

I used to think that last verse was a little strange. *You mean to say*, I thought, *that if I delight myself in the law of the*

Lord, he will even grant my dark and evil desires? No! If you actually *delight* yourself in his law, then you'll be delighted with the things that he wants. You'll be able to get rid of your dark and evil desires.

> But those who live in accordance with the Spirit have their minds set on what the Spirit desires. *Romans 8:5b*

> So I say, live by the Spirit, and you will not gratify the desires of the sinful nature. *Galations 5:16*

If you delight yourself in things that are an abomination to God, then obviously those are the things you will want, rather than the things that please God. Soon you'll have a difficult time telling which is which—and, of course, you'll be confused about his will.

In review: If you want to give God your mind, you must be willing to put a guard at the gate to protect you from "stinking thinking." Then you must *transform* that thinking by constant exposure to the Word of God.

That's Paul's advice, direct from the Bible: give God your body, give him your will, and give him your mind. If you want to know how God thinks and be confident that you're following his will, follow that advice.

God doesn't require that you spend an hour in fervent prayer, asking him which door you should use, before you leave the room. You don't have to spend months in agonizing doubt deciding what school he wants you to attend, or who he wants you to date, or what car he wants you to buy. You won't need to kill hundreds of sheep to lay out their fleeces, or make up other elaborate tests to find his will. Instead, give your body to God without reservation. Give your will to God by refusing to be pushed around by the world and by committing yourself to whatever he wants for your life. And last, give your mind to

Knowing the Will of God

God by refusing to dwell on things that will tempt you and drive you from him. Instead, saturate your mind with his Word.

Do this, and God will have what he wants most.

He Will Have You!

What does God want most? What is the most important aspect of his will? That he wants *you*. Body, mind, and will. If you're committed to him, if your heart is intent on pleasing him, then he will be a part of every decision you make. If you make the wrong decision, you can trust him to let you know.

As you seek God's will in your life, simply pray: "Lord, I have carefully considered the alternatives in making this decision. You know that I want more than anything else to do your will. You have my body, my mind, and my will. Thank you for watching over me as I make this decision and help me to stay dead center where you want me to be." Then make your decision, based on the facts that are available to you.

Then trust him. There's no need to second-guess yourself—or God. He won't let you down.

Romans 12:1–2 ends by saying this:

Then [after you've given God your body, refused to be compromised by the world, and transformed your mind to his way of thinking] you will be able to test and approve what God's will is —his good, pleasing and perfect will.

11~94